The Instant Guide to Healthy
Foliage Houseplants
Volume II

Series editor: David Longman

The Instant Guide to Healthy
Foliage Houseplants
Volume II

David Longman

Times
BOOKS

THE AUTHOR

David Longman is an expert in plant care who trained at the
Royal Horticultural Society's school at Wisley before joining his
long-established family firm of florists. A past Master of the
Worshipful Company of Gardeners, he is a Council member of
Interflora, a director of the Flower and Plant Council and a
regular exhibitor at the Chelsea Flower Show. He is General
Editor of this series.

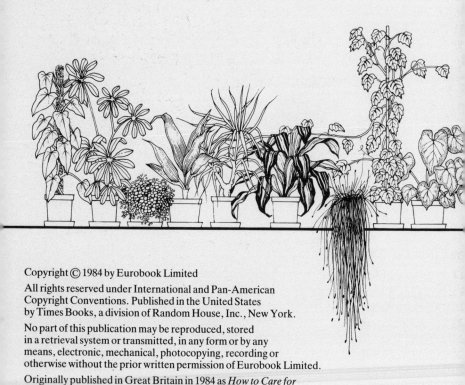

Originally published in Great Britain in 1984 as *How to Care for
More Foliage Houseplants* by Peter Lowe, London.

Library of Congress Catalog Card Number: 84-40634
International Standard Book Number: 0-8129-1174-1

Printed in Italy by Amilcare Pizzi SpA

9 8 7 6 5 4 3 2 1
First American Edition

Contents

Scientific names

Introduction

How to use this book

Most houseplants today are bought by their future owners rather in the same way that a picture or ornament is bought: to decorate a room. They are very necessary to soften the hard and often austere lines of modern furniture and decor. Unlike other decorative objects, however, plants are living things and need care if they are to survive and grow. Most come with instruction labels but these contain only brief hints and are often ambiguous. It is so easy to destroy in a few days what has probably taken the nurseryman months if not years to grow into a saleable specimen. This book, the second of two volumes on foliage plants in a comprehensive houseplant series is here to help you.

Foliage houseplants are those grown for the beauty of their leaves rather than for their flowers. Here each one is given a self-contained two-page entry. On the left is a general description of the plant with details of how to look after it, giving the correct amounts of water, light, warmth and humidity it needs, explaining how to clean and repot it and when and if it needs pruning. There is also a colour photo of a healthy leaf. On the right-hand page is a colour illustration of the plant showing all the things that can go wrong with it. Since this picture shows all the troubles at once, some of the plants look very sick indeed! To find out what is wrong with your plant, look for its symptoms on the illustration. Read the caption next to the part of the picture that shows the same features as your plant. It tells you what is wrong and how to put it right.

Different plants require different care and conditions, so whatever plant you acquire, make sure you read its detailed care instructions here and you will be able to look after it with confidence.

Tools for indoor gardening

It is possible to look after plants with the minimum of equipment a watering can, sprayer and plastic sponge are the real essential. However, for long-term houseplant care, you will need a much more comprehensive collection, which can be acquired gradually as the need arises.

Keep separate sprayers and watering cans for insecticides and fungicides and a stock of basic insecticides. Methylated spirits is useful for removing some pests. Mark all containers used for insecticides clearly and wash them out regularly.

Leafshine adds gloss but some plants react badly. These should be cleaned with a damp sponge or soft cloth, or with a fine mist spray. For delicate leaves use a feather duster or dry paintbrush. A paintbrush and cotton wool are useful for removing pests.

A small garden trowel and fork are useful when repotting or adding topsoil. A large spoon is a good substitute. A plastic bucket is essential for mixing composts, wetting peat and for giving very dry plants a thorough soaking.

Keep a selection of loam-based and peat-based composts, some pure moss or sedge peat. Some plants require lime-free mixtures. Sharp sand can be obtained from garden centres. Fertilizer, hormone rooting powder and charcoal are all useful.

Scissors, secateurs and a sharp knife are useful for removing dead or damaged leaves.

Two watering cans to which a rose can be attached are useful, one pint (½ litre) size, the other holding about a gallon (4½l). Never use your normal watering can for insecticides or fungicides.

Keep a small stock of flower pots and saucers, both plastic and clay. Old clay flower pots can be broken up to make excellent drainage material. Outer pots, with no drainage holes, can be used to hide the standard pot.

Twine, string, raffia and plant rings are essential for climbing plants, with a selection of canes, sticks and moss poles.

Watering and spraying

More houseplants are killed by incorrect watering (mainly of the little and often variety) than by anything else. Most prefer to be given a good soaking, then left almost to dry out before they are watered again. Some must be kept always moist – but in these cases the pot must be well drained so that the roots do not become waterlogged. Others prefer to dry out more thoroughly between waterings. Some need more water at one time of year than another. Always test the compost before watering to see how dry it is below the surface. In cold weather do not use cold water straight from the tap or the shock may damage the plant. Use tepid water for both watering and spraying.

Spraying keeps a plant's leaves clean and also provides extra humidity in hot, dry rooms. Avoid tap water if possible as the lime it contains clogs the pores of the leaves. Rainwater collected in a tank or bucket, water from melted ice in the freezer or boiled water which has been allowed to cool are all more suitable. Do not spray in bright sunlight as the water acts like a magnifying glass and may cause burn or scorch marks. A few plants dislike water on their leaves so before spraying you should check the individual requirements under each plant entry. Most, however, benefit from a fine mist spray.

Feeding

Most composts contain fertilizer but for healthy growth plants also need extra nourishment, usually in spring and summer. Houseplant food or fertilizer is available as a liquid, diluted before use, as a powder added to water, as granules scattered on the surface of the soil and as a pill or stick pushed into the soil and gradually absorbed. You can also obtain a foliar feed which is sprayed onto the leaves. For most houseplants a liquid food is most suitable. It is clean, has no smell, and is easy and economical to use. There are several brands available and it is a good idea to try several and to change from time to time. Normally

Watering

1. Test compost for dryness with finger or knife blade before watering. If blade comes out clean or soil dry and crumbly, compost is drying out. If soil sticks, it is still moist. Check instructions for each plant: some like a dry interval, others must be always moist.

2. Add water to top of compost, filling pot to the brim. Excess water will drain into saucer. After 15 minutes empty any water remaining in the saucer. Do not allow pot to stand in water.

3. If plant is very dried out and does not mind water on its leaves, plunge pot into bowl so that water covers pot rim. Spray leaves. Leave for 15 minutes, then take it out and allow it to drain.

4. If plant cannot tolerate water on its leaves, add water to fill the saucer and wait for 15 minutes for it to be absorbed. Empty excess so that plant does not stand in water.

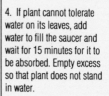

5. Or plunge pot into bowl or bucket of water to just below the pot rim. Leave it for 15 minutes, then take it out and allow it to drain.

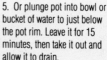

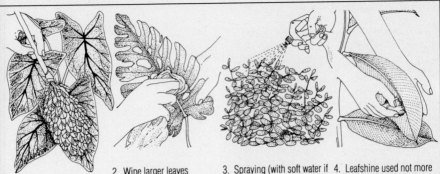

Cleaning the leaves

1. Flick very dusty plants with a feather duster before cleaning.

2. Wipe larger leaves with a damp cloth to remove dust and any insects such as red spider mite. Use soft water if possible. Remember to wipe the undersides of the leaves as well as the tops.

3. Spraying (with soft water if possible) is often enough to keep plants clean. The lime in hard water may mark the leaves and clog the pores. Do not spray in sunlight.

4. Leafshine used not more than once a month (not more than once every 2 months in some cases) brings a glossy shine to the leaves. Check instructions for your plant as some can be damaged by leafshine.

Humidity

Some foliage plants require higher humidity than is found in normal rooms, especially in dry, centrally heated homes. A group of plants will create its own more humid atmosphere but you can improve the humidity around them in several ways.

1. Spray regularly with soft water, holding spray about 6in (15cm) from plant. Do not spray in strong sunlight. Spray may mark or rot flowers, so check plant's requirements when in flower.

2. Put pebbles in plant's saucer and stand pot on top. Add water to saucer until it comes half way up the pebbles. Do not let bottom of pot touch water or plant will become waterlogged and roots will rot away. Water vapour will rise from the damp pebbles, providing extra humidity under the leaves. Add more water to saucer when pebbles begin to dry. A group of plants can be placed together on a tray of damp pebbles for even better local humidity.

3. Place pot inside a larger container and pack the space between the two with damp peat. Keep peat constantly moist. This is a good method to use if you have to leave the plants for some time as the peat will hold moisture well.

Pruning

Old plants may grow straggly and woody. Pruning back leggy stems in spring encourages new side shoots which give a more bushy, compact appearance. In general, cut stems down by half, just above a leaf or side shoot. But read individual instructions as some must never be pruned.

Old dead leaves should be cut off as close to the stem as possible. This encourages new young leaves to develop.

you can simply follow the instructions on the bottle, adding a few drops to the water in the can when watering. For some plants, however, the mixture must be weaker than the manufacturer recommends on the bottle. If it is used at too concentrated a strength, it will damage the roots. Never increase the recommended strength and be careful with tablets and fertilizer sticks. If they are too close to the roots, the concentrated fertilizer may cause root damage.

If in doubt, don't feed. It is always better to slightly underfeed than to overfeed – and never feed a sick plant.

Repotting

Plants need repotting either because the roots have totally filled the existing pot and can no longer develop or because the nutritional value of the compost has been used up. It's quite easy to tell if a plant needs repotting. Remove it from its pot (see right). If there is a mass of roots and no soil showing, it needs repotting – it is potbound. If any soil is visible, don't repot. Replace plant in its old pot and gently firm it back in position. Other signs are roots growing through the pot base and weak, slow growth. Newly purchased plants should not normally need repotting. Do not repot unhealthy plants: the shock may kill them. In fact if in doubt, don't repot.

Repotting is usually done in spring – March or April in the northern hemisphere, September or October in the southern. Most plants require good drainage so that water can run through the compost freely and air can get to the roots. Broken crocks from old clay flower pots or a layer of coarse gravel at the bottom of the pot will provide drainage. Never use a container without drainage holes in its base. Put a piece of paper or a layer of moss over the drainage crocks to stop the compost from blocking the holes and inspect the root ball for pests. Remove old stones, damaged roots and old soil and gently remove old, loose compost from the top to a depth of about ½in (1cm). Then place plant in new pot.

After repotting, leave the plant without

water for 2–3 days. The roots will spread out into the new compost in search of water. If it is very hot, spray the leaves every day.

Choosing the right compost: The correct type of compost or soil is very important for indoor plants. Don't use ordinary soil, which is usually too heavy and stifles the roots of young plants. Compost types vary considerably as some houseplants need a very light peat-based compost and some a heavy loam. The correct combination for each plant is given in the individual entries.

The two most commonly used types of compost are loam-based or peat-based. Loam-based compost is made up of sterilized loam (soil) mixed with peat and grit or coarse, washed sand. It is usually sold with fertilizer added, following formulae developed by the John Innes Institute for Horticultural Research. The numbers 1, 2 and 3 indicate the different proportions of fertilizer added. In this book they are referred to as 'loam-based No. 1, 2 or 3'.

Division

1. A many-stemmed plant that has grown bushy can often be divided into 2, 3 or even 4 new plants. First water plant and prepare as many smaller pots as you need – see Repotting.

3. Gently pull roots and stems apart with your hands. For a very pot-bound plant with mass of roots, use a sharp knife. Make sure all sections have portion of root and stem.

2. Remove plant from pot and shake away loose soil from around the root ball. Remove bits of gravel or stones.

4. Repot the divided sections into the new pots. Leave in shade, without water, for 2–3 days so that roots will grow into compost.

Taking cuttings

This is the most common way of propagating houseplants though seeds of some species are available.

First prepare a small pot with drainage and special rooting compost.

3. Dust the cut ends with hormone rooting powder.

5. Place in heated propagator or cover with polythene and keep in warm place (70°F, 21°C). Keep watered and remove cover for 5 minutes a day.

1. Choose a healthy stem tip or side stem and cut off the top 3–4in (8–10cm). Cuttings should include a growing tip and 2 pairs of healthy leaves.

2. Remove lowest pair of leaves and any side shoots from bottom part so there is a length of bare stem to insert into compost. Prepare other cuttings in the same way.

4. Make holes around edge of new pot. Insert several cuttings and firm compost gently round them. Water well.

6. When cuttings begin to grow (in about 4 weeks), pot singly in small pots.

Repotting

1. Prepare clean, dry pot not more than 2 sizes larger than old one. Place broken crocks or coarse gravel in bottom as drainage, then a piece of paper or moss and layer of new compost. Water plant well.

3. Remove damaged or dead roots with sharp knife.

5. Lower plant into new pot and add more compost round root ball, firming it with fingers or a round stick. Continue adding compost until pot is filled to within ½–¾in (1–1½cm). Leave without water in shade for 3 days.

2. Hold pot upside down as shown. Gently tap rim of pot on edge of table and remove pot with other hand. If pot sticks, tap in several places.

4. Gently break roots at bottom of ball and remove any bits of crock or stone. Remove all loose, old compost from top, to a depth of about ½in (1cm). Always handle with care so as not to damage leaves or buds.

6. For large plants in tubs carefully scrape away about 2–3in (5–7cm) old topsoil. Add new compost, leaving ½–¾in (1–1½cm) space between compost and pot rim. Firm down well and water, including feed.

Climbing plants

Some foliage plants are climbers and need to be trained up a cane or moss pole. Others need the support of a strong cane to keep their stems upright.

Canes

A single cane will support a tall plant or climber. Insert cane when repotting, after positioning plant but before adding all the compost. Cane should be a few inches from main stem, stopping about ⅔ down pot. If adding a cane at any other time, be careful not to damage roots as you push it in.

Insect-eaters

Insect-eating plants such as the Venus' Flytrap (*Dionaea muscipula*) trap and digest small flies that land on them. They are usually sold as very young, newly germinated plants in pots covered with a clear plastic top which provides them with a mini-greenhouse. This is ideal, for they are bog plants and need a very moist atmosphere. Keep them in good indirect light and well watered always. They can even stand in a saucer of water. They grow in ordinary room temperatures but prefer to be under 60°F (18°C) in winter, though not below 40°F (4°C). In summer they grow spikes of white flowers.

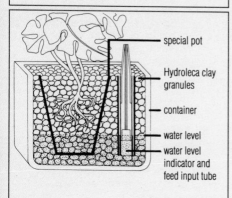

- special pot
- Hydroleca clay granules
- container
- water level
- water level indicator and feed input tube

Hydroculture

The art of growing plants in water is an easy way for the forgetful to enjoy indoor plants. The technique is relatively simple but has taken a long time to perfect. The plant is either grown as a cutting in water or converted (by a long process). The roots are held in position by granules of expanded fired clay which has no nutritional value.

The plant is fed by a special ion-exchange fertilizer which, over a long period, releases nutrients into the water. The chemicals in ordinary tap water activate the fertilizer and the plant takes it up through the roots as and when it needs nourishment. It is therefore not possible to over or underfeed a plant, provided that the fertilizer is renewed every 6 months. Making sure that the water is up to the right level as shown on the inbuilt water gauge is the only care required, except of course for an occasional dusting of the leaves. Overwatering, which kills so many plants, is impossible! Not all foliage plants are suitable but the range is wide. They are well worth buying and make ideal office plants.

Peat-based composts are more open in texture, sterile, and hold moisture longer. They are normally composed of 10 parts of peat to 1 part of coarse sand with fertilizer added in the same proportions as loam-based compost. It is important when using peat composts not to firm them into the pot too hard.

Ericaceous or lime-free compost is available for plants that do not tolerate lime. Sphagnum moss is useful for some plants which are grown on cork bark or for lining a hanging basket. Sharp sand is fine, washed sand, available from garden centres. Do not use coarse builders' sand. It is sometimes mixed with loam to give a specially well-drained compost. Other useful items are small polystyrene balls to lighten the soil texture, rotted leafmould and manure.

Mixing compost: If mixing your own blend of compost, put the different items into a plastic bucket, using the same measure for each one. A plant pot or old cup will do. For 2 parts loam, 1 part peat, for example, fill the measure twice with loam, then once with peat. Mix the items together well with a trowel or stick so that they are well blended.

Insecticides

Unfortunately some houseplants are vulnerable to pests and diseases. The most common are mealy bug, scale insect, red spider mite and green or whitefly. These should be treated as soon as they are noticed and affected plants moved away from others to prevent the spread of infection. Plants with thin, delicate leaves, are attacked by insects such as red spider mite while greenfly are attracted to young leaves and stems.

Insecticides are available usually as concentrated liquids which are added to water and sprayed or watered onto the infected plant, and as aerosols ready for use. Less usually, some chemicals for houseplants come in powdered form. This is not suitable for all plants – check the individual instructions. Systemic insecticides are absorbed into the plant's veins (its system) and so spread the poison to any insect which tries to take nourishment from these.

The least toxic insecticides are those based on pyrethrum and derris as these are both natural substances. They are most suited to whitefly and greenfly control. Derris is also suitable for whitefly and greenfly and controls red spider mite in the early stages. Methylated spirits can be used to remove scale insect and mealy bugs. Red spider can be prevented from recurring by improving humidity. Malathion is one of the most effective general insecticides and will control everything from whitefly to beetles, and especially mealy bug which is one of the most infectious and damaging insects likely to affect houseplants. Other insects such as scale insect and thrips can also be controlled by spraying malathion. It can be sprayed when diluted and also watered into the soil if the soil is infected.

Malathion may damage some sensitive plants, so read the captions carefully to make sure you choose the right treatment for your plant.

Air plants

These curious-looking plants grow naturally without soil. Most are *Tillandsia* (members of the Bromeliad family) and come from Central and South America. Their tiny root systems are used only for support and they live by taking moisture and nutrients from the air. They make ideal houseplants and are usually sold mounted on coral, sea shells, minerals or driftwood. Their care is simple. They should be kept in an airy position in good indirect or diffused light and sprayed daily in summer, every other day in winter, with a mist spray. Hold the spray about 1ft (30cm) from the plant and spray it lightly so that it dries out again within an hour. In summer add liquid houseplant food to the spray water once a month, diluting it to ¼ maker's recommended strength. They will stand a wide range of temperatures, down to 45°F (7°C) in winter — and any normal room temperature in summer.

Taking care with insecticides

Insecticides and fungicides may contain deadly chemicals. Use them with care.

Never mix different types of insecticides as the chemicals may react.

Never put them into other bottles, such as soft drink or beer bottles.

Never breathe in the spray.

Never spray in windy weather.

Never pour them down the sink or drains. Do not even pour the water in which you have washed containers and sprayers down the drain.

Never make up more at one time than you will use.

Never keep diluted insecticide for more than 24 hours.

Never leave old containers lying around.

Always follow instructions carefully. Do not over or under dilute.

Always use a separate watering can and sprayer, keeping another one for normal spraying and watering.

Always keep away from food, crockery, glasses, food containers, and minerals. Derris is harmful to fish; malathion harms bees.

Always cover fish bowls when spraying.

Always store them with their sprayers and containers in a dry, frost free place, on a high shelf out of reach of children.

Always spray outside, in the evening when bees are not around.

Always wash out all sprayers and empty bottles after use, inside and out.

Always pour washing water onto ground away from food crops and water sources such as streams and rivers.

Always throw empty bottles and containers away with domestic waste.

Always wash thoroughly in hot water and detergent when you have used them.

Pineapple

Ananas comosus

This is a striking houseplant whose shape and colouring contrast well in mixed plantings. Its brightly coloured leaves are, however, sharply toothed and .can easily scratch skin and tear clothing. It is a bromeliad but unlike many other plants of this type prefers to grow in normal soil not on bark or leafmould. Individual plants last only 2–3 years, but produce offsets after flowering which grow into new plants. All varieties will produce fruit though indoors there is rarely enough light (or space) for them to reach edible size.

Light: Full sunlight best but will survive in partial shade.
Temperature: Best at 65–70°F (18–21°C). If kept cooler, growth will be retarded – which can be good if in mixed plantings.
Water: Allow compost to dry out between waterings. Water once or twice a week in summer, once a week in winter.
Humidity: Benefit from high humidity. Spray overhead twice a week in summer, once a week in winter, more frequently if in hot dry room.
Feeding: Add liquid houseplant food at maker's recommended strength to water once a week in summer when growing or while fruit forming.
Soil: Likes rich compost – use loam-based No. 2.
Repotting: Repot at least twice while young rosette growing into proper plant, once 3 months after offset is separated, then again a year later when it is outgrowing its pot. But do not use too large a pot – one size larger each time. Do not firm compost down too hard – it prefers open texture. Wear gloves to protect hands from sharp leaves.
Cleaning: Wipe leaves if dusty with damp cloth. Do not use leafshine.

This small, compact Pineapple plant grows to 10–12in (25–30cm) high and the same across. Variegated ones fruit more slowly than plain green varieties and need full light all year round to keep the bright colour in their leaves. The larger *Ananas striatus* may reach 3ft (1m).

Burn marks on middle of leaves. Damage caused by spraying in sunlight. Plant needs humidity but do not spray while sun is on it. Remove unsightly leaf at base with sharp knife – wear gloves.

Rusty marks on leaves. Leafshine damage. Do not use. Clean only by wiping with damp cloth.

Propagation
Plant dies down after fruiting and a small offset grows beside it. When parent plant has shrivelled and offset is about half its size, remove both from pot and separate offset and roots with a sharp knife. Repot offset and keep moist at 70°F (21°C) for 21 days.

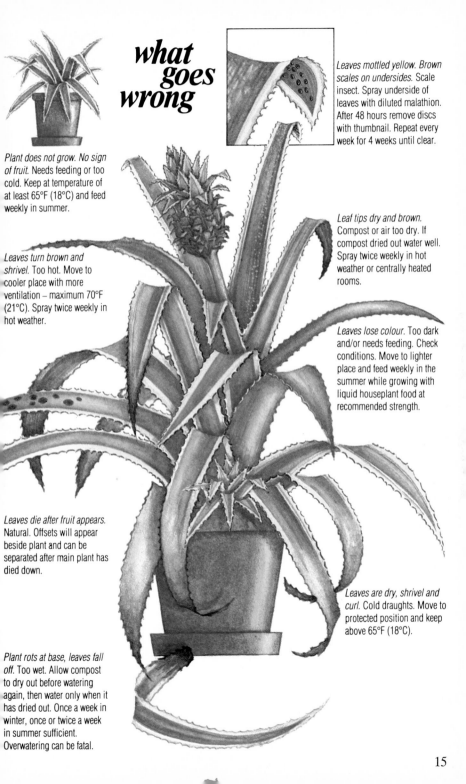

what goes wrong

Leaves mottled yellow. Brown scales on undersides. Scale insect. Spray underside of leaves with diluted malathion. After 48 hours remove discs with thumbnail. Repeat every week for 4 weeks until clear.

Plant does not grow. No sign of fruit. Needs feeding or too cold. Keep at temperature of at least 65°F (18°C) and feed weekly in summer.

Leaves turn brown and shrivel. Too hot. Move to cooler place with more ventilation – maximum 70°F (21°C). Spray twice weekly in hot weather.

Leaf tips dry and brown. Compost or air too dry. If compost dried out water well. Spray twice weekly in hot weather or centrally heated rooms.

Leaves lose colour. Too dark and/or needs feeding. Check conditions. Move to lighter place and feed weekly in the summer while growing with liquid houseplant food at recommended strength.

Leaves die after fruit appears. Natural. Offsets will appear beside plant and can be separated after main plant has died down.

Leaves are dry, shrivel and curl. Cold draughts. Move to protected position and keep above 65°F (18°C).

Plant rots at base, leaves fall off. Too wet. Allow compost to dry out before watering again, then water only when it has dried out. Once a week in winter, once or twice a week in summer sufficient. Overwatering can be fatal.

15

Aralia japonica

False castor oil plant

This is a very easy, quick-growing and large-leaved plant and will survive in quite dark positions. Its strong, glossy finger-shaped leaves can have a spread of up to 18in (45cm) across. It is tolerant of both low and high temperatures, and will even grow outside in temperatures down to but not below freezing. It does produce flowers, a cluster of white blooms in midsummer, but it must be in a very light position for these to appear. It is also known as *Fatsia* and is related to the elegant and more delicate *Aralia elegantissima*, the Finger Aralia.

The False castor oil plant may grow 3 to 5ft (1–1½m) high and across. The handsome leaves may be plain green or variegated with cream markings outlining the leaves. The variegated ones grow more slowly than the plain green ones.

Light: For best results needs full light but it will survive in dark corners away from natural light.

Temperature: Grows in a wide range from 32°F (0°C) in winter to 70°F (21°C) in summer.

Watering: Keep moist at all times in summer, watering at least twice a week. Once a week is enough in winter but check that compost never dries out completely.

Humidity: Mist spray daily in summer if temperatures near maximum, twice weekly in winter. Likes humidity.

Feeding: Add liquid houseplant food to water every 14 days in growing season, diluting to maker's recommended strength.

Soil: Loam-based No. 2.

Repotting: Repot once a year in spring as plant starts to produce new leaves. Use pot only one size larger. Plant prefers to have its roots constricted. If plant is growing straggly, stems can be cut back just above a leaf stem after repotting. Dab cut end with sulphur dust to prevent infection.

Cleaning: Regular mist spraying will keep leaves clean though they are large enough to wipe with a damp cloth. Use leafshine not more than once every 6 weeks.

Leaves distorted and sticky with green insects. Greenfly. Spray with pyrethrum-based insecticide or diluted malathion. Repeat weekly until clear.

Few new leaves grow, though feeding regular. Pot too large. Plant is growing roots, not leaves. Do not repot again for 2 years and always choose pot only one size larger than old one.

Webs under leaves with tiny red insects. Red spider mite. Remove webs with damp cloth or sponge, then spray with diluted malathion, especially under leaves. Repeat every 14 days until symptoms disappear. Improve humidity by standing pot on saucer of wet pebbles.

what goes wrong

Stems long and weak, long spaces between leaves. Too hot. Move to cooler, more airy place. Spray daily with soft, tepid water. Maximum temperature 70°F (21°C).

Whole plant droops. Waterlogged. Drain away any water in saucer and allow surface of compost to dry out before watering again. Then keep moist but never allow pot base to stand in water. Always throw away excess that drains through after watering and check plant has good drainage.

Leaves scorched and burned. Sprayed in sunlight. Spray in early morning or evening when sun not on leaves. Do not allow leaf tips to touch glass on sunny days.

Young leaves black. Frost; is plant behind curtains at night? Remove damaged leaves and move to warmer place over 34°F (1°C).

Leaves pale. Needs feeding. Feed every 14 days in growing season with liquid houseplant food diluted to maker's recommended strength.

Leaves limp. Air too dry in hot weather. Spray daily in summer, especially when near 70°F (21°C). In winter, spray twice weekly, more often if in hot, dry room.

Leaves droop. Compost too dry. Plunge pot into bucket of water for 10–15 minutes, then drain. Keep moist in summer and spray daily.

17

Cast iron plant

This is the toughest of all indoor plants. It is almost impossible to kill it without actually using poison, hence of course its common name. It was very popular in Victorian times, perhaps because it was the only plant that could stand the variable temperatures of most houses and the fumes from open coal fires and tobacco smoke. Variegated plants have handsome green and white striped leaves. A small purple flower appears occasionally out of the soil, growing quite separately from the leaves and lasting only a day or two. The plant likes to be slightly pot bound and should be kept on the dry side – though even consistent overwatering will rarely kill it.

Aspidistras or Cast iron plants, grow stems 10–12in (28–30cm) long. Although they are almost indestructible, and grow well in shaded corners, a little extra care will keep the elegant leaves bright and healthy.

Light: Will flourish in dark corners. Leaves may scorch in full sunlight.

Temperature: Normal room temperatures, 50°F–65°F (10–18°C).

Water: In winter about once a week (less if temperature below 50°F (10°C), in summer twice a week. Allow compost surface to dry out between waterings.

Humidity: Seems to like quite a dry atmosphere but an overhead mist spray once a week in summer is good.

Feeding: Do not overfeed. Once a month in summer with liquid houseplant food diluted to maker's recommended strength is enough. If leaves split, stop feeding for rest of season. Do not feed variegated plants.

Repotting: Prefers to be potbound, so repot every 3–4 years.

Soil: Loam-based No. 2 for plain green plants, seed compost or one without base fertilizer for variegated.

Cleaning: Wipe leaves with soft damp cloth when dusty. No leafshine.

Leaves pale. Compost exhausted and too dry. Repot in fresh compost and water more regularly. Do not allow to become bone dry between waterings. Once a week in summer, once a fortnight in winter correct.

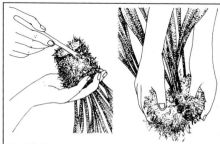

Root division

1. Divide in early spring if plant so crowded with stems that pot looks almost bursting. Remove from pot and tease away stale compost with a rounded stick.

2. Grasp rootball firmly and gently pull roots and stems apart, taking care not to damage either. Repot both parts in fresh moist compost but do not water again for 2 days.

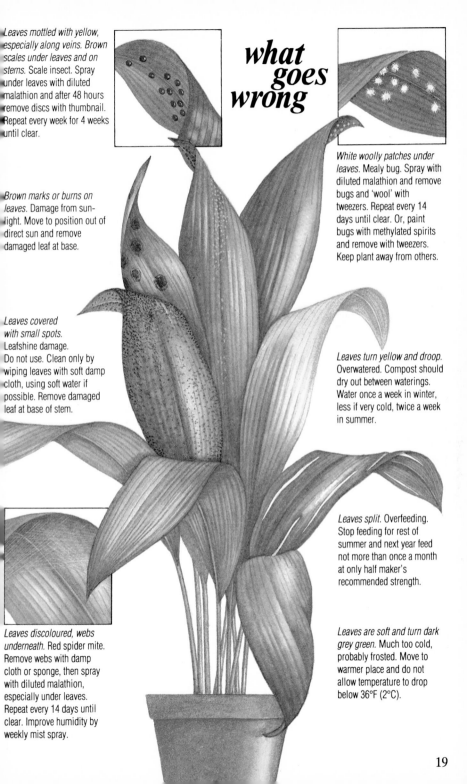

what goes wrong

Leaves mottled with yellow, especially along veins. Brown scales under leaves and on stems. Scale insect. Spray under leaves with diluted malathion and after 48 hours remove discs with thumbnail. Repeat every week for 4 weeks until clear.

White woolly patches under leaves. Mealy bug. Spray with diluted malathion and remove bugs and 'wool' with tweezers. Repeat every 14 days until clear. Or, paint bugs with methylated spirits and remove with tweezers. Keep plant away from others.

Brown marks or burns on leaves. Damage from sunlight. Move to position out of direct sun and remove damaged leaf at base.

Leaves covered with small spots. Leafshine damage. Do not use. Clean only by wiping leaves with soft damp cloth, using soft water if possible. Remove damaged leaf at base of stem.

Leaves turn yellow and droop. Overwatered. Compost should dry out between waterings. Water once a week in winter, less if very cold, twice a week in summer.

Leaves split. Overfeeding. Stop feeding for rest of summer and next year feed not more than once a month at only half maker's recommended strength.

Leaves discoloured, webs underneath. Red spider mite. Remove webs with damp cloth or sponge, then spray with diluted malathion, especially under leaves. Repeat every 14 days until clear. Improve humidity by weekly mist spray.

Leaves are soft and turn dark grey green. Much too cold, probably frosted. Move to warmer place and do not allow temperature to drop below 36°F (2°C).

19

Beaucarnea recurvata

Elephant foot tree

This unusual plant comes from Mexico and is best known as a houseplant in the United States but it is now becoming more available elsewhere. Its large swollen stem gives it its common name and in an old plant this stem may grow into an almost sculptured shape. On top is a bunch of palm-like leaves which droop attractively over the stem. It is well worth searching for as, given plenty of light, it is an attractive and trouble-free plant. It requires rather different conditions in summer and winter, needing warmth and moisture in summer but a cooler, drier period in winter. In centrally heated homes, keep it in the coolest room in winter, but with plenty of light.

The Elephant foot tree may grow to 6 ft (2 m) or more indoors, the stem lengthening gradually from its bulb-like base. The tuft of drooping leaves give it an alternative common name of the Pony tail plant.

Light: Best in full sun though will survive in more shady positions if moved into good light from time to time.
Temperature: In winter 50–55°F (10–13°C) best. In summer 70°F (21°C).
Water: Water 2–3 times a week in summer to keep soil always moist. Water once a week in spring and autumn and only every 3 weeks in winter, to give it a drier resting period.
Humidity: Spray once a week all the year round unless temperature below 50°F (10°C).
Feeding: Use liquid houseplant food at maker's recommended strength every 14 days in summer when plant is growing.
Soil: Loam-based No. 2.
Repotting: They do not like the roots to be disturbed, so every 2 years enough for young plant. For larger plants, change top 2–3in (5–7cm) soil in spring. Make sure drainage is always good.
Cleaning: Spraying will keep leaves clean or they can be wiped with damp cloth. Use leafshine not more than once a month.

White cotton wool patches on and under leaves. Mealy bug. Spray with diluted malathion and remove bugs and 'wool' with tweezers. Repeat every 14 days until clear. Or, paint bugs with methylated spirits and remove with tweezers.

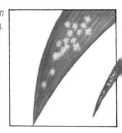

what goes wrong

Leaves droop and dry up. Too hot. Try to keep below 70°F (21°C), and spray weekly all the year round.

Brown scales under leaves. Scale insect. Spray underside of leaves with diluted malathion and, after 48 hours, remove scales with thumbnail. Repeat weekly for 4 weeks until clear. Or, paint scales with methylated spirits.

No new leaves appear and plant looks dull and tired. Needs feeding or too dark. Feed every 14 days in summer and keep in good light.

Burns on leaves. Caused by spraying in sunlight. Plant can stand direct sun but never spray when sun is on leaves. Remove unsightly leaf with sharp knife or scissors where it joins stem.

Stem shrinks and becomes gnarled. Soil too dry. Plunge pot into bucket of water for 10–15 minutes, then drain. Keep moist in summer and only allow surface to dry out in spring and autumn.

Leaves yellow and outer ones drop. Too wet, waterlogged. Drain away water in saucer and allow soil surface to dry out before watering again. Water 2–3 times a week in summer, once a week in spring and autumn. In winter allow soil to dry out completely between waterings – once every 3 weeks enough.

Leaves drop. Too cold. Keep above 50°F (10°C) and if temperature falls near minimum, keep compost dry, watering only once every 3 weeks in winter.

21

Tiger begonia

One of the most attractive of the small-leaved begonias, this has recently regained popularity. Grown widely in late Victorian and Edwardian times, it then virtually disappeared from commercial production until recently. It is ideal for hanging baskets, since it is compact and, though it trails naturally, rarely becomes too leggy. The flowers are small and yellow and the plant is grown mainly for its striking colouring.

Light: Good natural light but not direct sun.

Temperature: Winter minimum 55°F (13°C). Summer maximum 60–65°F (16–18°C).

Water: Twice weekly with soft water in summer, in winter about every 10 days to keep soil just moist. Water from top but do not get water on leaves.

Humidity: Spray every 3–4 days with fine mist in summer and stand pot on saucer of wet pebbles in hot weather. If temperature falls below 60°F (16°C) do not spray or stand on pebbles or leaves may become infected with mould.

Feeding: Every 14 days in growing season (spring and summer) with liquid houseplant food diluted to maker's recommended strength.

Soil: Light, open mixture of peat-based No. 2 compost or a mixture of 2 parts loam, 2 parts peat to 1 part leafmould and 1 part sharp sand.

Repotting: They do best in small pots (except when several plants are together in hanging basket) so repot only when roots look crowded. Take care not to damage delicate leaves.

Cleaning: Dust lightly with feather duster. Do not use leafshine. Do not wipe leaves or spray: leaves will mark.

The Tiger begonia's leaves are attractively marked with a pattern of lighter green and need good indirect light to look their best. They are one of the easier foliage Begonias and can be propagated by dividing roots and stems when new leaves start to appear in spring.

Propagation

This begonia can be propagated from stem cuttings or by dividing the roots and stems.

1. In spring, when new leaves start to show, prepare 2 clean pots with drainage and fresh compost. Remove plant from pot.

2. Gently pull roots and stems apart, being careful not to damage the leaves. Make sure that each section has both roots and stems.

3. Plant each section separately. Leave in shade without water for 2 days so that the roots spread out in compost to find water.

Leaves curl and go crisp at edges. Too hot. Move to cooler place with more ventilation, below 65°F (18°C). Provide extra humidity.

New leaves small in spring. Needs feeding. Feed with houseplant food diluted to maker's recommended strength every 14 days in spring and summer when growing.

New leaves dull with fine webs underneath. Red spider mite. Remove webs with damp cloth or sponge, then spray with diluted malathion, especially under leaves. Repeat every 14 days until clear. Improve humidity.

Leaves limp, plant droopy. Gas fumes. Move to fume-free room.

Leaves distorted with yellow rings and mottling. Mosaic virus. No cure. Destroy plant by burning if possible to avoid infecting others.

Grey-brown powdery patches on leaves. Too cold and damp. Spray with fungicide, then place in warmer position (above 55°F, 13°C) and spray less often. Allow compost surface to dry out between waterings. Remove damaged leaves at base of stem.

Brown patches on leaves. Caused by spraying water in sunlight. Use only fine mist spray in mornings and evenings. Small spots could be leafshine damage. Do not use.

Leaves small, lack colour, stems long and weak. Too dark. Move to lighter place but not direct sunlight.

what goes wrong

Leaves drop in winter. Too cold. Move to warmer place, above 55°F (13°C).

23

Angel wings

This is a beautiful but difficult plant belonging to the Arum family. Its leaves, almost paper-thin, are often white in background with veins marked in green, pink or red. They grow from a rhizome started into growth in heat in late winter and by spring are beginning to produce their long-stalked leaves. These continue to appear all summer, dying down again in late autumn. The rhizomes are difficult to keep through the winter and the plants are best treated as annuals. Great care must be taken not to overwater them as they soon rot if the temperature falls.

The Angel wing's leaves may be patterned and veined in white, green or pink. A small lily-like flower grows in summer but the spectacular leaves are the plant's main attraction. Take great care when moving these plants as stems and leaves bend and crack easily.

Light: Full light except midday summer sun needed to keep colour and contrast in the leaves.

Temperature: Between 60–65°F (16–18°C) in summer, maximum 75°F (24°C). Minimum in winter if you are keeping rhizomes 55°F (13°C).

Water: Keep always moist while in leaf, watering 2 or 3 times a week in hot weather. If temperature falls below 60°F (16°C) or leaves stop growing reduce watering. In winter keep dry.

Humidity: Do not spray overhead or leaves may be damaged. If possible stand with other plants as this gives more humidity.

Feeding: Feed every 21 days in growing season using liquid houseplant food at half maker's recommended strength.

Soil: Use 2 parts loam-based No. 2 to 1 part peat.

Repotting: Plant rhizomes in fresh compost after winter and do not disturb again for one year. Cover them with about their own depth of compost.

Cleaning: Light feather dusting only, no spraying, wiping or leafshine.

Overwintering

Stop watering when leaves die down and store in dry soil at 55°F (13°C). Or, remove from pots and keep in dry, dark place. Repot in spring, move to warmer place (65°F, 18°C) and start watering gradually to encourage new growth.

Leaves brown at edges, crisp. Slightly too cold. Move to warmer place, above 60°F (16°C).

Leaves and stems flop, curl up and die. Too cold. Move to warmer place, above 60°F (16°C) out of cold draughts. Leaves die down naturally in autumn.

Poor growth, leaves small. Too dark and/or needs feeding. Move to lighter place (plant takes full light except midday summer sun) and feed every 21 days in growing season with liquid houseplant food at half maker's recommended strength.

Humidity
Caladiums need humidity but spraying may damage leaves. Keep pot in outer pot filled with damp peat. Moisture from peat will rise under the leaves. But make sure drainage in plant pot is good so it does not get waterlogged.

what goes wrong

Leaves poor colour. Too dark. Move into good light, including full sun except at midday in summer.

Leaves dry up and shrivel. Too hot or compost too dry. Check conditions. Water immediately if compost feels dry, keeping always moist while in leaf. Keep below 75°F (24°C).

Leaves and stems distorted and sticky, with green insects. Greenfly. Spray with pyrethrum-based insecticide or diluted malathion. Repeat weekly until clear.

Leaves split and torn. Bad handling. Take great care when moving plant and do not wipe leaves.

Brown marks on middle of leaves. Damage by sunlight or leafshine. Move out of direct midday summer sun. Remove damaged leaf at base of stem.

Mould on stems and rhizomes. Too wet. Allow surface to dry out before watering again and never allow plant to stand in water. Keep above 60°F (16°C); if below this, allow surface to dry out between waterings.

Cissus antarctica

Kangaroo vine

This plant was first introduced to Europe in 1790 and must have been one of the first houseplants to be exported from Australia. If allowed to climb freely it will cover a wall and it can also be trailed from a hanging basket. In northern Europe particularly it is often used as a room divider and may grow 2–3ft (60–100cm) a year, clinging to a supporting trellis with its tendrils. It is a member of the vine family but indoors will produce neither flowers nor fruit. An easy plant for a beginner but keep it out of direct sunlight which will soon dry up the leaves.

The Kangaroo vine's oval leaves are slightly rough in texture. It climbs with tendrils, which soon attach themselves to wires, canes or a trellis. If it is growing too large it can be pruned severely in spring but the miniature variety, *C. striata*, may be more suitable for smaller rooms.

Light: Needs good indirect light. Best in a window that does not get direct sun. Do not keep more than 3–4ft (1m) away from a window.

Temperature: Keep at 55–60°F (13–16°C) in winter, 65–70°F (18–21°C) in summer. If temperature over 70°F (21°C) increase humidity.

Water: Twice a week in summer, every 14 days in winter sufficient. Check compost. It should dry out on surface between waterings.

Humidity: Spray weekly in summer. If temperature over 70°F (21°C), spray daily and stand pot on saucer of wet pebbles.

Feeding: Give liquid houseplant food every 14 days in summer, diluted to maker's recommended strength.

Soil: Loam-based No. 2.

Repotting: When plant is young and growing fast, will need repotting twice a year in mid-spring and midsummer. After 3 or 4 years just replace top soil and feed weekly in summer.

Cleaning: Regular spraying keeps plant clean but leafshine can be used every 2 months.

what goes wrong

Training
1. Cissus needs a cane to climb. Insert cane when repotting; at any other time be careful not to damage roots as you push it gently into compost.

2. Loop fine twine around cane and plant stem as shown, being careful not to bruise stem: knot should be against cane not stem. Or use special plant rings or ties.

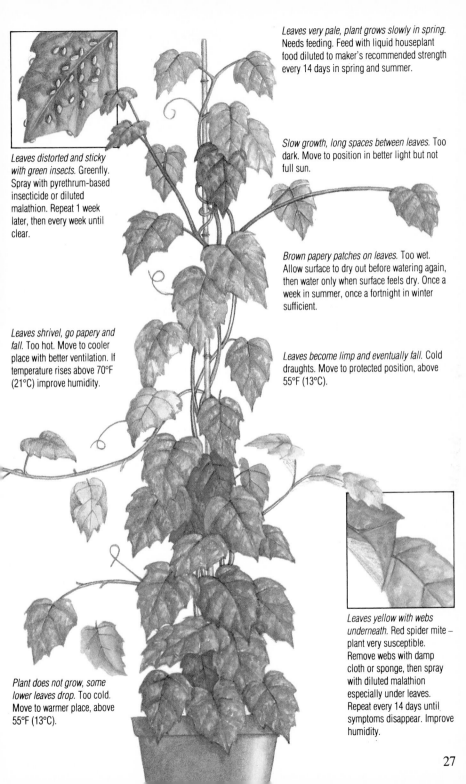

Leaves very pale, plant grows slowly in spring. Needs feeding. Feed with liquid houseplant food diluted to maker's recommended strength every 14 days in spring and summer.

Leaves distorted and sticky with green insects. Greenfly. Spray with pyrethrum-based insecticide or diluted malathion. Repeat 1 week later, then every week until clear.

Slow growth, long spaces between leaves. Too dark. Move to position in better light but not full sun.

Brown papery patches on leaves. Too wet. Allow surface to dry out before watering again, then water only when surface feels dry. Once a week in summer, once a fortnight in winter sufficient.

Leaves shrivel, go papery and fall. Too hot. Move to cooler place with better ventilation. If temperature rises above 70°F (21°C) improve humidity.

Leaves become limp and eventually fall. Cold draughts. Move to protected position, above 55°F (13°C).

Leaves yellow with webs underneath. Red spider mite – plant very susceptible. Remove webs with damp cloth or sponge, then spray with diluted malathion especially under leaves. Repeat every 14 days until symptoms disappear. Improve humidity.

Plant does not grow, some lower leaves drop. Too cold. Move to warmer place, above 55°F (13°C).

27

Cordyline terminalis

Flaming dragon tree

The Flaming dragon tree's bright red colouring makes it a popular houseplant. In fact its lower leaves tend to remain green and only the upper leaves are brightly coloured. Many varieties are grown, the favourite being 'Prince Albert' which grows to about 2ft (60cm) indoors. There is a slightly larger variety called 'Lord Robertson' and a miniature called 'Red edge' which, as its name suggests has red-edged leaves, growing to only about 5in (13cm) long. Not a plant for the novice, but a good one if you have a little experience. Cordylines are closely related to Dracaenas (pp.34–37) and there is often confusion in naming the varieties.

The Flaming dragon tree has dark green leaves, spectacularly splashed with red and purple. Buy plants with bright leaves growing right down to the bottom of the stem unless the plant is growing on a thick cane, when there should be a bunch of healthy leaves at the top.

Light: They need strong light to maintain colour but keep away from direct midday sun. Green varieties tolerate shade.
Temperature: To maintain growth and colour keep at 65–70°F (18–21°C). Will stand down to 55°F (13°C) if kept almost dry. Maximum summer temperature 75°F (24°C). If higher, increase mist spraying to improve humidity.
Water: Keep always moist, watering once or twice a week in summer, depending on temperature, once a week in winter.
Humidity: Spray twice weekly in summer and winter but never in direct sunlight. If over 75°F (24°C), spray daily.
Feeding: Add liquid houseplant food at maker's recommended strength to water every 14 days during growing season.
Soil: Either loam-based or peat-based No. 2.
Repotting: Every other year enough. Always ensure drainage hole is clear.
Cleaning: Wipe leaves with damp cloth. Leafshine may be used once a month except on 'Red edge' variety.

Pruning
1. If your plant has lost its lower leaves and stem looks bare, you can prune it to make it shoot new leaves further down stem.

2. Cut stem just above a leaf scar with secateurs or a sharp knife. Dust tip with fungicide to prevent infection and keep stem under polythene bag to give extra humidity.

3. New leaves will sprout from further down the stem to give a better balanced shape.

what goes wrong

Leaves lack colour. Not enough light. Move into position of good diffused light but not strong midday summer sun.

Leaf edges brown or spots on leaves. Damage caused by spraying in sunlight. Needs humidity but do not spray while sun is on leaves. Remove unsightly leaf at base of stem.

Leaves yellow with webs underneath. Red spider mite. Remove webs with damp cloth or sponge, then spray with diluted malathion, especially under leaves. Repeat every 14 days until symptoms disappear.

Leaves distorted and sticky with green insects. Greenfly. Spray with pyrethrum-based insecticide or diluted malathion. Repeat 1 week later, then weekly until clear.

New leaves small and distorted. Needs feeding. Feed with liquid houseplant food at maker's recommended strength every 14 days in the growing season.

Brown scales under leaves and on stems. Scale insect. Spray with diluted malathion and, after 48 hours, remove discs with thumbnail. Repeat weekly for 4 weeks until clear.

Leaves shrivel and dry up. Too hot. Keep below 75°F (24°C) if possible and if temperature near maximum provide extra humidity.

Leaf tips turn brown, lower leaves drop. Air too dry. Spray plant twice weekly with soft, tepid water and if over 75°F (24°C) stand on wet pebbles for extra humidity.

Leaves rot and drop off, no new ones appear. Too cold or too wet. Check conditions. Move to warmer place, above 60°F (16°C), and if compost waterlogged, allow surface to dry out before watering again. Always test compost before watering.

29

Ctenanthe oppenheimiana

Never-never plant

This beautiful foliage plant is a distant relative of the Marantas (p. 44) but grows in a more upright manner. It is also sometimes sold as a Calathea. A native of Brazil, its name comes from the Greek word for comb and refers to the shape of the flower which is only produced on mature plants. Another species, *Ctenanthe lubbersiana*, is also sometimes available. This has plainer leaves, mottled with light green or cream and is a rather tougher plant.

The Never-never plant's leaves turn at right angles, parallel to the ground. A healthy plant may reach 3ft (90 cm) with 15in (33cm) long leaves, though most plants on sale are only around 12in (30cm) tall.

Light: They do not like strong light and should not be in a window that receives full midday or afternoon sun. Will survive well in shade but will benefit from more light in winter.

Temperature: Best above 60°F (16°C) in winter but will survive down to 50°F (10°C) if compost kept almost dry. Up to 80–85°F (27–29°C) in summer if humidity kept high.

Water: Compost must be kept very moist at all times. Water 2–3 times a week in summer, once a week in winter. If around 50°F (10°C) in winter, water only every 10–12 days.

Humidity: Need high humidity to flourish. Spray daily in summer, twice a week in winter. Place pot on saucer of wet pebbles for constant local humidity.

Feeding: Feed every 14 days in growing season (summer) using liquid houseplant food at half maker's recommended strength.

Soil: Peat-based No. 2 compost, must be open, porous mix.

Repotting: Once a year in late spring. Make sure drainage is good and do not press compost down too much.

Cleaning: Spraying will keep leaves clean; if very dusty wipe with damp cloth. No leafshine.

Brown scales under leaves and on stems. Scale insect. Spray underside of leaves with diluted malathion and, after 48 hours, remove discs with thumbnail. Repeat every week for 4 weeks until clear. Or paint with methylated spirits.

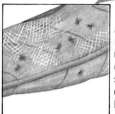

Leaves lose colour and have webs underneath. Red spider mite. Remove webs with damp cloth or sponge, then spray with diluted malathion, especially under leaves. Repeat every 14 days until clear. Improve humidity.

30

Leaves pale and small. Needs feeding. Feed with liquid houseplant food at half maker's recommended strength in summer growing season.

Plant collapses. Soil too dry or waterlogged. If dry, plunge pot into bucket of water for 10–15 minutes, then drain. If soil wet and dark, allow to dry out before watering again.

Leaves curl and wither. Too hot, air too dry. Spray daily in summer and stand pot on wet pebbles, especially if temperature over 80°F (27°C).

Leaves curl up and do not open. Too cold or too much light. Check conditions. Move out of strong sunlight and keep above 60°F (16°C).

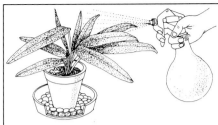

Humidity
Never-never plants need constant high humidity and moist soil. Place pot on saucer of pebbles half covered in water but do not allow pot base to stand in water or roots will rot. In hot weather spray every day and water whenever soil begins to dry out.

Leaves lose colour. Too dark. Does not need full light but must not be too shaded. In winter, move to light position.

what goes wrong

Rust marks on leaves. Leafshine damage. Do not use. Clean only by spraying with soft tepid water. Remove damaged leaf at base of stem.

Leaves droop and look limp. Too hot. Move to cooler place, below 80°F (27°C) if possible and spray daily to keep humidity high.

Dieffenbachia amoena

Dumb cane

Now that plant breeders have introduced new, more compact and stronger varieties, this plant has rightly increased in popularity. A member of the Arum family it was first introduced from Brazil in 1830, being grown first in the Imperial Palace in Schönbrunn, Austria, by the head gardener, Herr Dieffenbach. Take care when handling it as the sap is poisonous, causing swellings if it touches the mouth or lips. Always wash your hands after touching it and wear gloves for pruning. Smaller plants do well in mixed groups but the larger ones are best standing alone.

Light: Good indirect light. Darker leaved plants tolerate semi-shade but if too dark, they will grow longer, less healthy stems.
Temperature: Prefers 60–65°F (16–18°C) but for short periods will stand down to 50°F (10°C), though this may cause loss of some lower leaves. If over 75°F (24°C) increase watering and humidity.
Water: 2 or 3 times a week in summer, with rainwater if possible, to keep compost moist. In winter not more than once a week, allowing compost to dry out if temperature falls below 60°F (16°C).
Humidity: Spray overhead in summer, daily when near 75°F (24°C); stand pot on wet pebbles or use in mixed planting for extra humidity.
Feeding: Feed monthly in spring and summer with houseplant food diluted to maker's recommended strength.
Repotting: In spring each year. Move to pot 2 sizes larger each time as plants may grow over 12in (30cm) a year.
Soil: Loam-based No. 3.
Cleaning: Sponge leaves every 14–21 days, supporting them carefully as they snap easily. Use leafshine only once a month.

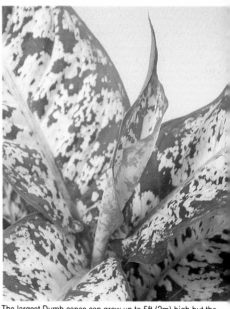

The largest Dumb canes can grow up to 5ft (2m) high but the smaller plants, varieties of *Dieffenbachia picta*, are unlikely to grow more than 3ft (1m) high. The markings vary from plant to plant and new varieties have increasingly large areas of cream.

Cleaning the leaves
Dumb cane leaves snap easily so support them gently when cleaning. Wipe carefully with damp cloth or sponge every 2 or 3 weeks. The sap is dangerous so always wash your hands after touching plant and wear gloves if cutting any part of it.

what goes wrong

Leaves small and plant grows lanky. Too dark. Move into good indirect light, not strong sunlight.

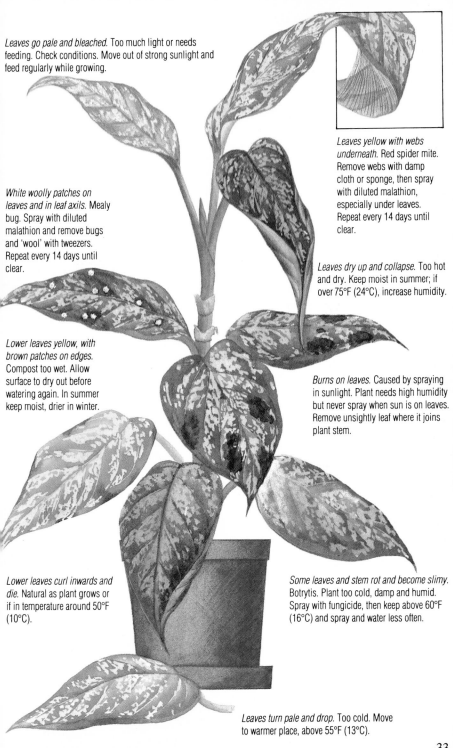

Leaves go pale and bleached. Too much light or needs feeding. Check conditions. Move out of strong sunlight and feed regularly while growing.

Leaves yellow with webs underneath. Red spider mite. Remove webs with damp cloth or sponge, then spray with diluted malathion, especially under leaves. Repeat every 14 days until clear.

White woolly patches on leaves and in leaf axils. Mealy bug. Spray with diluted malathion and remove bugs and 'wool' with tweezers. Repeat every 14 days until clear.

Leaves dry up and collapse. Too hot and dry. Keep moist in summer; if over 75°F (24°C), increase humidity.

Lower leaves yellow, with brown patches on edges. Compost too wet. Allow surface to dry out before watering again. In summer keep moist, drier in winter.

Burns on leaves. Caused by spraying in sunlight. Plant needs high humidity but never spray when sun is on leaves. Remove unsightly leaf where it joins plant stem.

Lower leaves curl inwards and die. Natural as plant grows or if in temperature around 50°F (10°C).

Some leaves and stem rot and become slimy. Botrytis. Plant too cold, damp and humid. Spray with fungicide, then keep above 60°F (16°C) and spray and water less often.

Leaves turn pale and drop. Too cold. Move to warmer place, above 55°F (13°C).

33

Dracaena marginata

Madagascar dragon tree

This narrow-leaved Dracaena makes a splendid feature, especially when an old plant is pruned to give several heads of young leaves on top of a gnarled, almost 'bonsai' like trunk. It is an easy plant to grow and is tolerant of most conditions, though the colour of the leaves is better in good light. Dracaenas are a large family of plants, most of which make good houseplants. Some, such as the Madagascar dragon tree are commonly sold with stems ready formed. Others, such as *Dracaena deremensis* and *D. fragrans massangeana* (see p.36) may be purchased before the woody stem has developed.

The Madagascar dragon tree has narrow leaves edged with red which grow from the top of a thin, woody stem. They are usually around 18–24in (46–60cm) tall and their palm-like shape is an interesting contrast to other foliage plants. A pretty variegated type with green and white leaves is more delicate.

Light: Keep in good light but away from direct sun. If too dark, leaves lose colour.
Temperature: In winter 60°F (16°C), but will stand 55°F (13°C) if water withheld. Summer maximum 75°F (24°C).
Water: Water twice a week in summer, once a week in winter to keep moist but not waterlogged. Must never dry out completely.
Humidity: Spray with tepid water 2–3 times a week, only once a week in winter. Do not spray if below 55°F (13°C).
Feeding: Feed every 14 days in the growing season (spring and summer) with liquid houseplant food diluted to maker's recommended strength.
Soil: Peat or loam-based No. 2.
Repotting: Every other year in spring. When too large to handle easily, just replace top 2–3in (5–7cm) compost with fresh.
Cleaning: Wipe leaves with damp cloth. Use leafshine once a month but too much will clog pores and slow down new growth.

Leaves yellow with spots and underneath, webs. Red spider mite. Remove webs with damp cloth or sponge, then spray with diluted malathion, especially under leaves. Repeat every 14 days until symptoms disappear. Improve humidity by standing pot on wet pebbles.

what goes wrong

Leaves dull and droopy. Too hot and air too dry. Keep below 75°F (24°C) if possible and spray 2–3 times a week in summer. Drooping bottom leaves may be caused by sudden change in temperature. Plant should recover if kept above 60°F (16°C).

Plant flops, leaves turn yellow and rot. Roots rot. Too wet, waterlogged. Drain away any water in saucer and allow surface to dry out before watering again. Then keep moist but never allow to stand in water. Always throw away excess after watering.

Leaves discoloured with brown scales. Scale insect. Spray underside of leaves with diluted malathion and, after 48 hours, remove discs with thumbnail. Repeat every week for 4 weeks until clear. Or, paint with methylated spirits.

Brown scorch marks on leaves. Caused by spraying in sunlight. Do not spray if sun on leaves. Remove unsightly leaf where it grows from trunk.

Leaves lose colour. Too dark. Move to lighter position, but not in direct sunlight.

New leaves small, slow growth. Needs feeding. Feed every 14 days in spring and summer, with houseplant food at maker's recommended strength.

Stem rots from top, leaves drop. Too cold. Move to warmer place, above 60°F (16°C).

White woolly patches on leaves and stems. Mealy bug. Spray with diluted malathion and remove bugs and 'wool' with tweezers. Repeat every 14 days until symptoms disappear. Or, paint with methylated spirits, remove with tweezers. Keep away from other plants.

Lower leaves droop, curl under, edges yellow, tips brown. Too dry. Plunge pot into bucket of water for 10–15 minutes, then drain. Keep moist in summer, watering every day if it dries out. In winter water once a week to keep drier.

35

Dracaena

Like the Ficus and Philodendron groups of plants, Dracaenas include a large number of different species, many of which are among the most popular of indoor plants. They range from species that will stand a mild frost to others that are at home in tropical jungle conditions. Members of the Lily family, their scientific name comes from the Greek word for a female dragon and many include the word dragon in their popular names. All Dracaenas have similar shaped strap-like leaves, growing as a rosette from a central stem which gradually elongates. The different types vary in colour and size. *Dracaena massangeana* (or *D. fragrans massangeana*) grows indoors to 2–3ft (60–90cm).

The Belgian evergreen or Ribbon plant (*Dracaena sanderiana*) is another of the popular Dracaenas. It grows to about 3ft (90cm) indoors, its slender green and white leaves unfurling one above the other around the stem. In time the lower leaves fall, leaving a bare, cane-like stem.

Light: Best in good light but out of midday summer sun; will tolerate 2–3 weeks in a shady place.

Temperature: Will survive in minimum 55°F (13°C) but better at 65°F (18°C). If over 75°F (24°C) in summer, increase humidity and fresh air.

Water: Once a week in winter, at least twice a week in summer but never let plant stand in water or roots will rot.

Humidity: Spray twice weekly, more often if temperature near maximum, using rainwater if possible.

Feeding: Give liquid houseplant food at maker's recommended strength every 14 days in spring and summer.

Soil: Loam- or peat-based No.2.

Repotting: In spring annually while young. For plants over 4 years old, repot every second or third year. Make sure drainage is good.

Cleaning: By hand with damp cloth. Use leafshine not more than once a month.

Leaves go pale and fade. Too dark. Move to a lighter position.

what goes wrong

Leaves yellowed with webs underneath. Red spider mite. Remove with damp cloth or sponge, then spray with diluted malathion, especially under leaves. Repeat every 14 days until symptoms disappear. Improve humidity by standing on a saucer of pebbles almost covered in water.

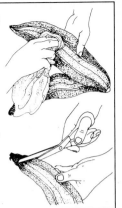

Plant collapses, leaves go rotten – so may stem and root. Plant waterlogged, standing in water. Drain away any water in saucer and allow surface of soil to dry out before watering again. Then keep moist but never allow pot base to stand in water. Always throw away excess that drains through after watering.

Plant drops lower leaves and stops growing. Too cold. Move to warmer place. Do not allow temperature to drop below 55°F (13°C).

New leaves small, and slow growth in spring. Needs feeding. Feed with houseplant food diluted to maker's recommended strength every 14 days in spring.

Leaves discoloured with brown scaly insects which are under leaves and on stems. Scale insect. Spray underside of leaves with diluted malathion and, after 48 hours, remove discs with thumbnail. Repeat every week for four weeks until clear.

Burn spots on leaves. Damage caused by spraying in sunlight. Plant needs high humidity but must not be sprayed when sun is shining on it or droplets will act like magnifying glasses and burn leaves. Remove unsightly leaf with sharp knife where it joins stem.

Greyish brown spots on leaves. Botrytis. Plant too cold and damp. Spray with fungicide, then keep in warmer place (above 60°F, 18°C) and spray with water less frequently. Allow soil surface to dry out between waterings. Remove damaged leaves.

Lower leaves drop. Much too dry and hot. Water more frequently and increase spraying.

Ficus elastica

Rubber plant

This is still one of the most popular of all houseplants for it will grow and flourish in most homes with the minimum care. It is a native of India, where it grows to a 100ft (30m) tree but indoor varieties have been bred to grow more compactly, with smaller leaves. Take care not to break the leaves or cut the stem or they will 'bleed'. If this happens, seal the wound immediately with cotton wool or tissue dipped in petroleum jelly. Two other large-leaved *Ficus* species make good specimen plants: *F. lyrata*, the Fiddleback fig and *F. benghalensis*, the Banyan fig.

The Rubber plant's glossy leaves are about 10in (25cm) long and 6in (15cm) across when fully grown. New leaves appear at the plant's tip, covered at first by a protective sheath which falls away as the leaf unfurls. If the tip is removed, the plant should branch.

Light: Will stand some shade but will not grow so well. Keep out of direct sunlight.
Temperature: Winter minimum 60°F (16°C), summer maximum 85°F (29°C).
Water: Do not overwater – if in doubt, leave it another day or two and never leave standing in water. Water only when compost feels dry, twice a week in summer, once a week or less in winter. In winter use tepid water.
Humidity: Spray at least once a week, more often if over 70°F (21°C).
Feeding: Feed every 14 days in spring and summer when growing with liquid houseplant food diluted to maker's recommended strength.
Soil: Loam-based No. 2. Make sure it is well drained.
Repotting: Repot once a year in spring, more often if plant is growing quickly and needs larger pot to keep it stable. When too large to handle, replace top 2–3in (5–7cm) compost and feed every 10 days in summer.
Cleaning: Wipe with damp cloth, supporting leaves carefully. Use leafshine not more than once a month.

Air layering

1. If your plant has lost its lower leaves but the top is still growing, use air layering to improve its appearance. With sharp knife make shallow cut in stem below leaf or leaf scar. Insert small stone and dust cut with hormone rooting powder.

2. Wrap damp moss or soft, absorbent paper around cut, tie firmly and wrap polythene round to seal in moisture.

3. When new roots grow from cut, slice off stem below them and repot top in fresh compost. Discard lower stem or seal top with petroleum jelly and it may reshoot.

Leaves pale, new ones small and distorted. Needs feeding. Feed every 14 days in spring and summer while growing.

Leaves pale. Too much light. Move to more shaded spot, out of direct sunlight.

Yellow spots on leaves, webs underneath. Red spider mite. Remove webs with damp cloth or sponge, then spray with diluted malathion, especially under leaves. Repeat every 14 days until clear. Improve humidity.

Brown scales under leaves and on stems. Scale insect. Spray underside of leaves with diluted malathion and, after 48 hours, remove discs with thumbnail. Repeat every week for 4 weeks. Or, paint with methylated spirits.

Burns on leaves, especially after spraying. Caused by spraying in sunlight. Keep out of strong sun and never spray in sunlight. Remove leaf and stem.

Leaves hang down, curl and seem limp. Too dry. Plunge pot into bucket of water for 10–15 minutes, then drain. Allow surface to dry out between waterings but check regularly in hot weather and in centrally heated rooms.

what goes wrong

White woolly patches on leaves. Mealy bug. Spray with diluted malathion and remove bugs and 'wool' with tweezers. Repeat every 14 days until symptoms disappear. Or, paint bugs with methylated spirits, remove with tweezers.

Bottom leaves turn yellow, droop and fall. Too wet. Allow to dry thoroughly before watering again and in winter use tepid water. Very old plants lose lower leaves naturally.

Leaves from any part of plant drop suddenly. Brown patches on other leaves. Too cold. Move to warmer place, above 60°F (16°C).

39

Canary ivy

These large-leaved ivies are very popular as houseplants. They are not quite as hardy as the smaller-leaved *Hedera helix* (see other books in this series on Foliage and Windowbox and Balcony plants) and will not survive outside in frost. They need plenty of light, and high humidity especially in winter but must never be overwatered. Unless they are well staked, they tend to look untidy and if not pruned grow straggly. Pinch out the growing point once or twice a year for a more bushy plant. They are very susceptible to red spider.

Hedera canariensis 'Gloire de Marengo' is the most common of the large-leaved ivies. Another attractive plant is 'Golden leaf' which has two shades of green on its leaves and often reflects a gold tint in bright light. Like all variegated plants, the colour of the leaves improves if kept in good light.

Light: Best in strong light but not midday summer sun or leaves may be bleached.
Temperature: Winter minimum 45°F (7°C), summer best at 60–65°F (16–18°C). If above this, increase humidity.
Water: Water twice a week in summer, once a week in winter. Allow surface to dry out between waterings.
Humidity: Spray every day in summer or in centrally heated rooms; once a week enough if near winter minimum. For constant humidity, stand pot on saucer of wet pebbles.
Feeding: Every 14 days while growing in spring and summer, using liquid houseplant food diluted to maker's recommended strength.
Soil: Loam- or peat-based No. 2.
Repotting: Young plants grow quickly and need repotting twice a year. When over 2 years old, repot once a year in spring. When too large to handle, replace top 2–3in (5–7cm) soil annually.
Cleaning: Regular spraying will keep them clean but if very dusty, wipe leaves with damp cloth. Use leafshine not more than once a month.

Canary ivy is very susceptible to red spider mite attacks, especially in hot, dry rooms. Keep humidity high by regular spraying and stand pots on wet pebbles for extra local humidity.

what goes wrong

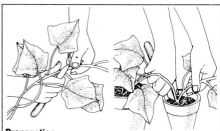

Propagation
1. Prepare small pot and place next to plant. Choose vigorous stem and cut a slit on lower surface just below a leaf. Place cut stem against compost in new pot and peg closely down.

2. Keep moist. Roots grow from cut and when these are visible and tip has signs of new growth, cut stem with sharp knife to separate plants.

Leaves distorted and sticky with green insects. Greenfly. Spray with pyrethrum-based insecticide or diluted malathion. Repeat weekly until clear.

Leaves have brown tips and patches. Soil and air too dry. Water immediately by plunging pot into bucket of water for 10–15 minutes, then drain. Spray daily in hot weather and stand pot on saucer of wet pebbles.

Leaves curl and look dark. Too cold. Keep above 45°F (7°C) in winter. Will not survive frost.

Leaves black all over plant. Waterlogged. Drain away any water in saucer and allow surface to dry out before watering again.

Leaves yellow with webs underneath. Red spider mite. Remove webs with damp cloth or sponge and spray with diluted malathion, especially under leaves. Repeat every 14 days until symptoms disappear. Increase humidity.

Leaves discoloured with brown scales. Scale insect. Spray underside of leaves with diluted malathion and, after 48 hours, remove discs with thumbnail. Repeat weekly for 4 weeks until clear.

Leaves pale and bleached. Too much sunlight or needs feeding. Or, too dark. Check conditions and move to position in good indirect light. Feed every 14 days in spring and summer with houseplant food at maker's recommended strength.

Leaves dry and crisp. Too hot. Move to cooler more airy place and spray daily in summer. Try to keep below 65°F (18°C).

Silvery marks on leaves. Thrips. Spray with diluted malathion or systemic insecticide every week until clear.

Black sooty patches on leaves. Sooty mould. Wipe off with mild diluted household disinfectant.

41

Mind-your-own-business

This bright green plant grows almost like a weed in a greenhouse but is a useful plant in a bowl or trough. It is a mass of tiny round leaves which grow on very thin stems and quickly hide any ugly exposed soil or edging. It is a relative of the nettle, comes from Corsica and is very easily propagated by division in spring. It likes a cool, moist position and will not do well where there are gas fumes. It is sometimes called *Soleirolia soleirollii*. A similar and related plant is *Nertera depressa*. This grows more slowly but in late summer and autumn is covered with tiny orange berries. It, too, needs very moist conditions.

Mind-your-own-business is an excellent plant for covering bare patches of compost in a trough or large pot; take care to plant it only with other moisture loving species, though, as it needs to be kept very damp all the year round.

Light: Grows in most positions although is most vigorous in good indirect light. Keep away from direct sunlight after watering. Will tolerate shade.

Temperature: Minimum in winter 45°F (7°C), summer maximum 70°F (21°C). May burn in summer if in direct sun.

Water: Keep moist at all times, watering 3–4 times a week in summer, once a week in winter. Never let it dry out.

Humidity: Spray daily if temperature over 70°F (21°C), otherwise once a week is sufficient.

Feeding: Not really necessary but if fed every 14 days with liquid houseplant food diluted to maker's recommended strength, it will grow faster.

Soil: Loam-based No. 2.

Repotting: Repot in spring. It is best to divide plant before repotting. Separated pieces quickly form compact new plants.

Cleaning: The leaves are too small to wipe but spraying should keep them dust-free. No leafshine.

Plant shrivels, leaves hang down. Soil too dry. Plunge pot into bucket of water for 10–15 minutes, then drain. Keep always moist in summer, watering every day if it dries out in hot weather. Do not allow to stand in water. Spray regularly.

Leaves turn black in winter. Too cold. Move to warmer place, above 40°F (4°C).

Plant wilts. Too hot and dry. Move to cooler place, below 70°F (21°C). Water and spray immediately.

Root division

1. These plants grow rapidly to cover the pot with foliage and it is best to divide them each year to keep them to a manageable size. Do this in spring, before repotting. First prepare 2 pots with drainage and layer of loam-based No. 2 compost. Water plant.

2. Remove plant from pot and tease away excess soil from around roots with a rounded stick or pencil.

3. Gently pull stems and roots apart, leaving a good section of both roots and stems on each half.

4. Repot each one separately and leave in shade without water for 2 days to encourage roots to explore new compost.

Leaves covered with small insects which fly out when plant is moved or touched. Whitefly. Spray with pyrethrum-based insecticide or diluted malathion. Repeat weekly until clear.

Rusty marks spotting leaves. Leafshine damage. Do not use. Clean only by spraying with soft, tepid water. Remove damaged leaf at base of stalk.

what goes wrong

Leaves turn yellow and die. Plant waterlogged, standing in water. Likes to have moist soil but must not stand in water or roots will rot. Make sure drainage is good. Always check soil before watering, especially in winter when it will not dry out so quickly.

Burns on part of foliage. Damage by strong sunlight. Move into area of good indirect light, out of harmful rays of sun. Remove damaged leaves at base of leaf stalks.

Maranta leuconeura

Prayer plant

This plant belongs to one of the most decorative families of houseplants. All have beautifully marked leaves, some looking almost as if they have been hand painted. Originating from the tropics, they need high humidity and often do best in bowls of mixed plants where a more humid atmosphere is created. The common name comes from the way that at night the young leaves curl up and seem like fingers clasped together in prayer. Some varieties are also known as 'Rabbit's tracks'.

Maranta leuconeura tricolor is the most decorative of all the Marantas or Prayer plants. Its beautifully coloured leaves have a soft, velvety bloom and need high humidity to keep them fresh and bright. Never try to make them more glossy with leafshine.

Light: Best in indirect light, away from a sunny window. In summer they do well in shade but in winter need more light.

Temperature: Will survive down to 50°F (10°C) if soil allowed to dry out between waterings but do better above 60°F (16°C). In summer up to 80–85°F (27–29°C) provided humidity is kept high.

Water: Keep moist at all times unless temperature down to 50°F (10°C). Water 2–3 times a week in summer, once a week in winter, every 10 days if around 50°F (10°C).

Humidity: High. Spray daily in summer, twice weekly in winter. If not in mixed planting, keep pot on wet pebbles.

Feeding: Add liquid houseplant food to the water every 14 days in spring and summer while growing, diluting food to half maker's recommended strength.

Soil: Need an open, porous mix. Peat-based No. 2 is good.

Repotting: Repot once a year in spring but do not firm compost down too hard. In mixed plantings, just change top 1in (2½cm) soil annually.

Cleaning: Spraying will keep it clean but if dusty, wipe leaves carefully with damp cloth. No leafshine.

Leaves limp, brown and patchy with curled edges. Too wet. Drain away any water in saucer and allow compost surface to dry out before watering again. Keep soil moist but not waterlogged. If temperature falls to 50°F (10°C), water only every 10 days.

what goes wrong

Leaves fade, webs underneath. Red spider mite. Remove webs with damp cloth or sponge, then spray with diluted malathion, especially under leaves. Repeat every 14 days until symptoms disappear. Improve humidity by standing pot on saucer of wet pebbles and spray regularly.

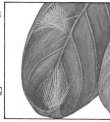

Root division

1. Large plants with many stems and a large rootball can be divided in early spring, just as new leaves start to grow.

2. First prepare 2 clean pots with drainage and compost.

Remove plant from pot and tease old compost from roots with rounded stick.

3. Grasp the rootball firmly and gradually pull it apart, making sure each section has both roots and stems.

4. Repot both sections separately, do not firm soil down too hard around roots. Leave without water for 2 days in a shady place. This allows roots to spread out in search of water. Move back into good indirect light and start watering again as usual.

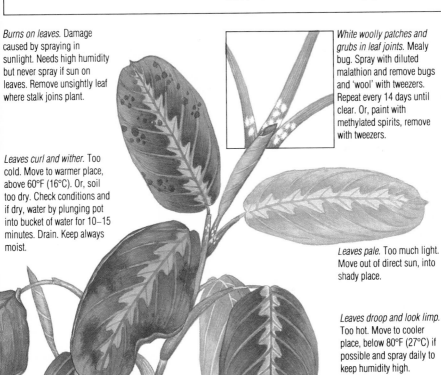

Burns on leaves. Damage caused by spraying in sunlight. Needs high humidity but never spray if sun on leaves. Remove unsightly leaf where stalk joins plant.

Leaves curl and wither. Too cold. Move to warmer place, above 60°F (16°C). Or, soil too dry. Check conditions and if dry, water by plunging pot into bucket of water for 10–15 minutes. Drain. Keep always moist.

White woolly patches and grubs in leaf joints. Mealy bug. Spray with diluted malathion and remove bugs and 'wool' with tweezers. Repeat every 14 days until clear. Or, paint with methylated spirits, remove with tweezers.

Leaves pale. Too much light. Move out of direct sun, into shady place.

Leaves droop and look limp. Too hot. Move to cooler place, below 80°F (27°C) if possible and spray daily to keep humidity high.

Leaves lose colour and look lifeless. Too dark and/or needs feeding. Check conditions. Move to lighter place (but not direct sunlight) and feed every 14 days in growing season with houseplant food diluted to half maker's recommended strength.

Monstera deliciosa

Swiss cheese plant

One of the most handsome of the larger houseplants, this is easy to grow and very tolerant of varying temperatures. It does, however, need a lot of space if it is to show the full beauty of its deeply cut leaves. It eventually produces an edible, but to western tastes not very appetising fruit. It should always be grown up a moss pole or sturdy stake, otherwise it will spread out horizontally. An easy plant for a beginner who wants something large and showy. It grows slowly but will reach a height of 8ft (230cm) after many years.

Light: Avoid direct sunlight; does well away from windows, in shade.

Temperature: Will survive down to 50°F (10°C) in winter but prefers no lower than 55°F (13°C). In summer easily up to 75°F (24°C), higher if humidity increased.

Water: Do not overwater – allow to dry out between waterings. Once a week sufficient in summer unless temperature over 70°F (21°C); every 14 days in winter. Always check soil before watering to see that surface is dry.

Humidity: Spray 2–3 times a week in summer, once a week in winter. Use soft water if possible. Stand pot on wet pebbles.

Feeding: Do not overfeed. Add liquid houseplant food at maker's recommended strength to the water every 3 weeks in summer.

Soil: Porous, peat-based No. 3.

Repotting: Once a year in spring. When too large to handle easily, replace top 2–3in (5–7cm) of soil with fresh. Always support plant with stake or moss pole.

Cleaning: Wipe leaves with damp cloth, supporting carefully from underneath. Use leafshine once a month.

In the wild, the Swiss cheese plant grows in very windy regions and the dramatic holes and splits in its leaves may help to prevent wind damage. The aerial roots which grow from the stem are essential to the plant's health and should never be cut off.

Leaves have brown tips. Too dry. Water immediately, then check compost weekly. Surface should dry out in summer but will do this more quickly when temperatures are high.

Leaves pale with webs underneath. Red spider mite. Remove webs with damp cloth or sponge, then spray with diluted malathion, especially under leaves. Repeat every 14 days until symptoms disappear. Improve humidity.

Lower leaves yellow, then brown especially in winter. Too wet. Allow soil surface to dry out thoroughly before watering again, then water only about once every 14 days so that compost dries out between waterings.

46

Plant does not grow. Too dark. Needs some indirect light to flourish. If in very dark corner, provide artificial lighting.

Some leaves do not split. You have a plant called 'Philodendron pertusum' which shares the same common name. It will not grow so large.

what goes wrong

Leaves badly torn and split. Human damage. Move plant to position where it will not be knocked.

Black patches on leaves. Too cold. Move to warmer place, above 55°F (13°C).

Brown marks on centre and edges of leaves in summer. Damage caused by spraying in sunlight. Never spray when sun is on leaves. Remove leaf if badly marked, cutting stalk where it joins main stem. Use sharp knife.

Leaves turn pale. Needs feeding. Feed every 3 weeks in summer while new leaves growing.

White woolly patches where leaves join stem. Mealy bug. Spray with diluted malathion and remove bugs and 'wool' with tweezers. Repeat every 14 days until symptoms disappear.

Leaves dry up and shrivel. Soil and air too dry. Water well and spray 2–3 times a week in summer. Check compost regularly when temperatures are high.

Polynesia

An attractive creeping plant that is moderately easy to grow and does well in hanging baskets. Two species are normally grown, *Pellionia pulchra*, also known as the Rainbow vine, and *P. daveauana*. The first has rounded, silvery green leaves with dark markings along the veins. The second has more pointed leaves with a lighter central area. Slow growers, they need careful watering in winter or they may rot. If a plant becomes leggy and loses its leaves near the centre, it is best to repropagate and start again. Cuttings taken in summer root easily.

The Polynesia plant's leaves change as they age from dull red to silvery green, marked with darker green along the veins. The young leaves are delicate and may be easily bruised if handled carelessly.

Light: Does well in shady position, but prefers indirect light away from direct sunlight.

Temperature: Minimum 60°F (16°C) in winter. Up to 80°F (27°C) in summer. Increase humidity if temperature rises too high.

Water: Keep moist at all times, unless temperature drops to minimum. Do not overwater or allow pot to stand in water; twice a week in summer, once a week in winter enough.

Humidity: Likes a humid atmosphere. Spray daily when over 70°F (21°C) in summer, once a week in winter when under 65°F (18°C).

Feeding: Every 21 days in spring and summer with liquid houseplant food at maker's recommended strength.

Soil: Likes an open compost, so use peat-based No. 2.

Repotting: Once a year in spring. Young leaves are tender, take care not to bruise them.

Cleaning: Spraying should keep it clean. Do not use leafshine.

Little green flies and sticky substance on leaves.
Greenfly. Spray with pyrethrum-based insecticide or diluted malathion. Repeat one week later and every week until clear.

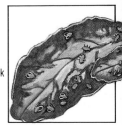

Cuttings
1. Take cuttings in summer if plant has grown leggy. Cut off stem tip 2–3in (5–8cm) long, including growing point and at least 2 pairs of leaves.

2. Trim off stem below leaf, remove lower leaves and dust end with hormone rooting powder. Insert in mixture of sand and peat, cover with polythene and keep warm until rooted.

Leaves limp, plant collapses. Compost too dry. Water immediately. Allow compost surface to just dry out before watering again. In winter water sparingly only once a week.

what goes wrong

Leaves pale, perhaps with scorch marks. Too much direct sun. Move to position in good indirect light.

Leaves go crisp and spotted. Leafshine damage. Do not use. Clean only by spraying with soft tepid water. Remove damaged leaf.

Grey mould in winter on stems near base. Botrytis. Plant too cold and damp. Spray with fungicide, then move to warmer place, over 60°F (16°C) and spray with water less frequently. Allow surface to dry out between waterings. Remove damaged leaves.

Stems rot, leaves collapse. Compost too moist. Allow surface of soil to dry out before watering again, then water only after surface has dried out. Twice a week in summer, once a week in winter should be enough but test compost before watering.

Leaves and stems go crisp and leaves drop off. Too hot. Move to a cooler place with more ventilation. Spray daily with soft, tepid water. Maximum temperature 80°F (27°C).

Plant grows leggy and drops leaves. Too dark. Move to lighter place (but not direct sunlight).

49

Peperomia magnoliaefolia

Desert privet

Desert privet plants have thick, fleshy leaves, rather like succulents. Unlike true succulents, however, they need a shady position since in the wild they grow at the foot of or in large trees. There are many varieties available. *Peperomia magnoliaefolia* is the most popular but others include *P. caperata*, with indented, dark green leaves, *P. hederifolia* with pale grey leaves and, most striking of all, *P. sandersii* or *argyreia* which has smooth green, silvery striped leaves on bright red stems. *P. magnoliaefolia's* first leaves are plain green, the variegated green and cream markings appearing as the plant grows.

The Desert privet's green and cream leaves make it attractive all the year round. A small, compact plant, it rarely grows to more than 8in (20cm) high. Some varieties produce flowers which grow in upright spikes rather like mouse tails and are usually off white in colour.

Light: Keep away from direct sun, but not in half darkness: indirect light best.
Temperature: Between 60–65°F (16–18°C) in winter, though will survive down to 50°F (10°C) for short periods if kept dry. Summer maximum 75°F (24°C).
Water: Allow to dry out between waterings: every 10 days in summer, every 14–18 days in winter enough. Overwatering, especially in winter, can cause rotting and botrytis.
Humidity: They like a humid atmosphere so spray twice a week in summer and winter unless temperature below 60°F (16°C). Stand pot on wet pebbles for extra humidity.
Feeding: Give liquid houseplant food every 14 days in spring and summer, diluting to half maker's recommended strength.
Soil: Loam-based No. 1.
Repotting: In spring only if outgrowing pot. They have small root system and do better in small pots.
Cleaning: Spraying sufficient. If wiping with a damp cloth, take care as leaves are brittle. No leafshine.

Leaves shrivel, dry up and die. Too hot. Move to cooler room, below 75°F (24°C).

Parts of leaves and base of stem go black and rot. Too wet. Allow soil to dry out before watering again, then water less often. Once every 10 days in summer, once every 14–18 days enough in winter.

what goes wrong

Leaves drop. Too cold. Move to warmer place, above 60°F (16°C).

Plant does not grow and looks dull. Needs feeding. Feed with liquid houseplant food diluted to half maker's recommended strength every 14 days in spring and summer.

Leaves dull and pale. Too much light. Move out of strong sunlight, into more shady place.

Rust spots on leaves. Leafshine damage. Do not use. Clean only by spraying or wiping leaves with damp cloth. Remove damaged leaf where it joins stem.

Cuttings

1. Take stem tip cuttings in spring. Cut off stem with 2 pairs of leaves and growing tip. Trim below bottom leaves.

2. Remove lowest pair of leaves and dip stem in hormone rooting powder. Plant in sand/leafmould and keep covered at 65°F (18°C) for 21 days.

Leaves yellow with webs underneath. Red spider mite. Remove webs with damp cloth or sponge, then spray with diluted malathion, especially under leaves. Repeat every 14 days until symptoms disappear. Improve humidity.

Leaves look blistered. Waterlogged, may be standing in water. Drain away any water in saucer and allow surface to dry out before watering again. Always throw away excess from saucer after watering.

Grey mould on stems. Botrytis. Too cold and damp. Spray with fungicide, then move to warmer room and spray with water less often. Winter minimum best above 60°F (16°C). Allow soil surface to dry out between waterings. Remove damaged leaves where they join stem.

Leaves limp. Compost and air too dry. Water immediately by plunging pot into bucket of water for 10–15 minutes, then drain. Spray twice a week all the year round unless temperature falls below 60°F (16°C).

51

Climbing philodendron

Philodendrons are a very large family of plants, many of which make excellent houseplants. They are generally divided into upright and climbing types – the upright ones are covered in this book's companion volume. Many new varieties of climbing Philodendron have been specially bred as houseplants; all need the support of canes or moss poles and most grow quickly into large, handsome plants. The large leaved types have pointed leaves that are mainly green but may be so dark as to be nearly black, red or almost golden. Growing up to 2–3ft (60–100cm) a year, they make ideal plants for office or showroom displays.

Large-leaved climbing Philodendrons, like this *Philodendron erubescens* 'Emerald Queen' are quick growers, making up to 2–3ft (60–100cm) a year in good conditions. Strong support from a cane or moss pole is essential.

Light: Best in indirect light (not direct midday sun) but will survive in semi-shade.
Temperature: In winter 55–65°F (13–18°C); in summer up to 75°F (24°C).
Water: Keep moist in summer, watering regularly twice a week while growing. Allow soil surface to dry out in winter, watering once a week.
Humidity: Spray twice weekly all the year round; in winter use tepid water.
Feeding: Feed every 14 days in growing season (spring and summer) using liquid houseplant food at maker's recommended strength.
Soil: Loam or peat-based No. 2.
Repotting: Young plants need repotting at least once a year in spring. When they have grown too large to handle easily, replace top 2–3in (5–7cm) compost each year with fresh and feed regularly.
Cleaning: Wipe leaves with a damp cloth. Use leafshine not more than once a month.

Making a moss pole
1. Choose cane long enough to reach to top of plant from pot base and tie a piece of string about 9in (22cm) from end.

2. Take enough sphagnum moss to cover rest of cane and loosen it with stick or pencil. Bind moss along cane with string, tying off at top with a firm knot.

3. Position cane when repotting and tie plant loosely to pole in several places.

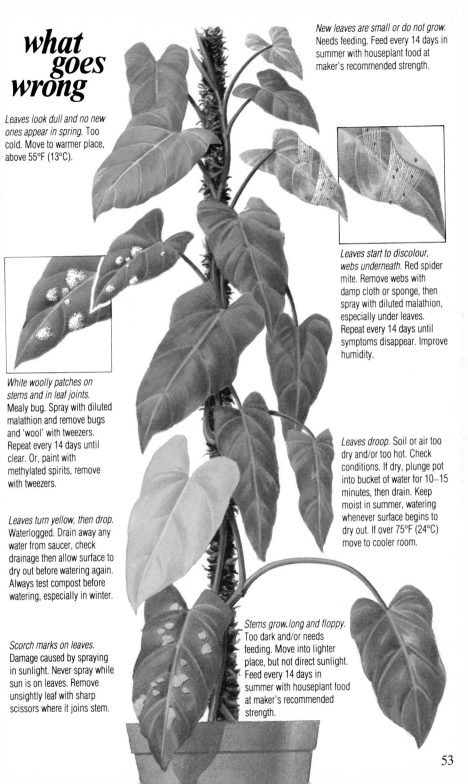

what goes wrong

Leaves look dull and no new ones appear in spring. Too cold. Move to warmer place, above 55°F (13°C).

New leaves are small or do not grow. Needs feeding. Feed every 14 days in summer with houseplant food at maker's recommended strength.

Leaves start to discolour, webs underneath. Red spider mite. Remove webs with damp cloth or sponge, then spray with diluted malathion, especially under leaves. Repeat every 14 days until symptoms disappear. Improve humidity.

White woolly patches on stems and in leaf joints. Mealy bug. Spray with diluted malathion and remove bugs and 'wool' with tweezers. Repeat every 14 days until clear. Or, paint with methylated spirits, remove with tweezers.

Leaves turn yellow, then drop. Waterlogged. Drain away any water from saucer, check drainage then allow surface to dry out before watering again. Always test compost before watering, especially in winter.

Leaves droop. Soil or air too dry and/or too hot. Check conditions. If dry, plunge pot into bucket of water for 10–15 minutes, then drain. Keep moist in summer, watering whenever surface begins to dry out. If over 75°F (24°C) move to cooler room.

Scorch marks on leaves. Damage caused by spraying in sunlight. Never spray while sun is on leaves. Remove unsightly leaf with sharp scissors where it joins stem.

Stems grow long and floppy. Too dark and/or needs feeding. Move into lighter place, but not direct sunlight. Feed every 14 days in summer with houseplant food at maker's recommended strength.

53

Sweetheart plant

This plant comes from the West Indies and is the most popular of all the Philodendrons. It grows rapidly, requires minimum care and does reasonably well in darker areas. When growing well it will soon cover a trellis with its dark green, heart-shaped leaves. Being a vigorous climber it needs supporting at all times, and has small aerial roots which will attach themselves to whatever is used. Recently it has been grown as a trailing plant for hanging baskets but if grown like this, keep it bushy by pinching out the leading shoots 2 or 3 times in summer. It also does well in hydroculture.

The Sweetheart plant has heart-shaped leaves some 4–5in (10–12cm) long which should be a strong, bright green. Avoid plants that look leggy or have yellowing leaves. This small-leaved species can be either trained as a climber or allowed to trail from a hanging pot.

Light: Keep away from direct sunshine but otherwise will stand most positions. Grows best in a window that does not receive direct sun.

Temperature: Winter minimum 65°F (18°C) though will survive down to 55°F (13°C). Summer maximum 75°F (24°C).

Water: Twice a week in summer while growing. In winter keep drier, watering once a week or less. Always test compost before watering to check that surface has dried out.

Humidity: Spray overhead twice a week all year round. In winter use tepid water.

Feeding: In summer feed with liquid houseplant food every 14 days, diluting to maker's recommended strength.

Soil: Loam or peat-based No. 2. Make sure compost is porous.

Repotting: Repot once a year in spring until too large to handle easily. Then simply replace top 2–3in (5–7cm) soil, being careful not to disturb roots. Make sure pot has good drainage.

Cleaning: Wipe leaves with damp cloth. Use leafshine not more than once a month.

Changing the topsoil

1. When plant is too large to remove from pot, carefully scrape away 2–3in (5–7cm) compost from top of pot.

2. Add fresh compost leaving ½–¾in (1–2cm) between compost and rim to allow space for watering.

3. Firm compost around roots with palms and water well. Add liquid food to water to replace nutrients and continue to feed every 14 days during the growing season.

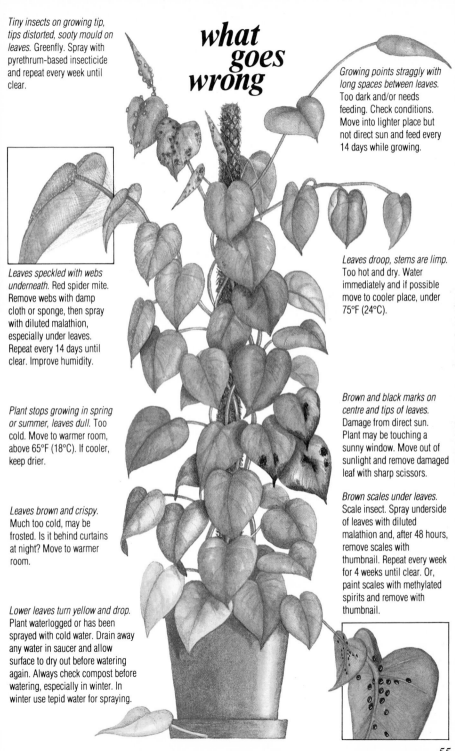

what goes wrong

Tiny insects on growing tip, tips distorted, sooty mould on leaves. Greenfly. Spray with pyrethrum-based insecticide and repeat every week until clear.

Growing points straggly with long spaces between leaves. Too dark and/or needs feeding. Check conditions. Move into lighter place but not direct sun and feed every 14 days while growing.

Leaves speckled with webs underneath. Red spider mite. Remove webs with damp cloth or sponge, then spray with diluted malathion, especially under leaves. Repeat every 14 days until clear. Improve humidity.

Leaves droop, stems are limp. Too hot and dry. Water immediately and if possible move to cooler place, under 75°F (24°C).

Plant stops growing in spring or summer, leaves dull. Too cold. Move to warmer room, above 65°F (18°C). If cooler, keep drier.

Brown and black marks on centre and tips of leaves. Damage from direct sun. Plant may be touching a sunny window. Move out of sunlight and remove damaged leaf with sharp scissors.

Leaves brown and crispy. Much too cold, may be frosted. Is it behind curtains at night? Move to warmer room.

Brown scales under leaves. Scale insect. Spray underside of leaves with diluted malathion and, after 48 hours, remove scales with thumbnail. Repeat every week for 4 weeks until clear. Or, paint scales with methylated spirits and remove with thumbnail.

Lower leaves turn yellow and drop. Plant waterlogged or has been sprayed with cold water. Drain away any water in saucer and allow surface to dry out before watering again. Always check compost before watering, especially in winter. In winter use tepid water for spraying.

Pittosporum tenuifolium

Australian laurel

This green-leaved plant is often associated with cut flowers in winter for it is the standard foliage used by most florists. However, it makes a good, shrubby or tree-like indoor plant, especially in its variegated form. It needs plenty of light but does well in cool winter temperatures, so is well suited to a porch, sun-room or conservatory. Its small, pale green leaves grow close together on woody stems and in summer it grows rapidly. In the wild Pittosporums grow up to 30ft (10m) high and even indoors may need pruning in spring to keep them to a manageable size. Cut stems just above a leaf.

Australian laurels grow over 3ft (1m) indoors and need very good light, full sun if possible. The leaves are familiar to many people who have never seen them growing as a houseplant since they are widely used as foliage in florists' displays.

Light: Must be in a very light position and will take full sun. Will drop its leaves if too dark.

Temperature: Minimum winter temperature 40°F (4°C) and even slight frost if protected by polythene. Up to 75°F (24°C) in summer but requires plenty of air and high humidity if indoors.

Water: Keep moist at all times, watering 2–3 times a week in summer – once a week in winter. If down to minimum temperature do not water at all.

Humidity: If in central heating in winter or if over 70°F (21°C) in summer spray daily. In other circumstances spray twice a week.

Feeding: Every 14 days in growing season using liquid houseplant food at maker's recommended strength.

Soil: Loam-based No. 2. They need heavy loam to hold them upright.

Repotting: When young repot every spring. When too large to handle easily, replace top 2–3in (5–7cm) as new leaves start to grow.

Cleaning: The spraying should keep it clean, but leafshine can be used once a month.

Leaves are limp and hang down. Soil too dry. Plunge pot into bucket of water for 10–15 minutes, then drain. Keep constantly moist in summer, watering every day if it dries out in hot weather. Do not allow to stand in water. Spray daily with soft, tepid water.

White woolly patches under leaves. Mealy bug. Spray with diluted malathion and remove bugs and 'wool' with tweezers. Repeat every 14 days until symptoms disappear. Or, paint bugs with methylated spirits and remove with tweezers.

Leaves pale and drop off. Not enough light. Move to a position in diffused daylight but not direct sun.

Leaves droop and turn yellow. Too wet, overwatered. Allow surface to dry out before watering again. If temperature below 40°F (5°C), keep dry. Otherwise water 2–3 times a week in summer, once a week in winter.

what goes wrong

Humidity
Pittosporums need constant humidity. Spray them daily in hot weather and stand pot on saucer of pebbles or gravel half covered in water. Do not allow pot base to rest in water or compost will waterlog and roots rot.

Young leaves go black. Too cold. Move to warmer place. Do not allow temperature to drop below 40°F (4°C).

Variegated leaves lose markings. Too dark. Move into good light. Will stand full sunlight.

Plant does not grow in summer. Needs feeding. Feed with houseplant food at maker's recommended strength every 14 days in spring and summer.

Spots on leaves that look like burn marks. Damage caused by spraying in sunlight. Plant needs high humidity but must not be sprayed when sun is shining on leaves. Remove unsightly leaf with scissors where it joins stem.

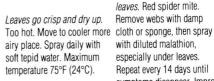

Leaves go crisp and dry up. Too hot. Move to cooler more airy place. Spray daily with soft tepid water. Maximum temperature 75°F (24°C).

Leaves fade, with webs and small insects underneath leaves. Red spider mite. Remove webs with damp cloth or sponge, then spray with diluted malathion, especially under leaves. Repeat every 14 days until symptoms disappear. Improve humidity.

Swedish ivy

This plant has been used as a house-plant almost from the beginning of indoor gardening but has never become very common. Though its leaves look ordinary, it makes a lovely hanging basket plant and produces delicate mauve flowers from the end of trailing stems in late autumn/early winter. Its pale green leaves are faintly aromatic and must be handled with care as they snap or break easily. It is a native of Australia. Other varieties include one with variegated leaves and one with darker green leaves.

Swedish ivy has pale green serrated, slightly aromatic leaves which must be handled with care as they snap and break easily. Grown mainly for its trailing foliage, it produces delicate mauve flowers in late autumn/early winter.

Light: Best in a window that does not receive midday summer sun; tolerates some shade.

Temperature: Up to 70–80°F (21–27°C) in summer. Winter minimum 55°F (13°C).

Water: Water thoroughly twice a week in summer, once a week in winter so that soil surface dries out well between waterings. Remember to check hanging baskets regularly as they dry out quickly.

Humidity: Will survive in normal room humidity but a twice weekly spray helps to keep them clean and bright.

Feeding: Give liquid houseplant food every 21 days in summer at half maker's recommended strength.

Soil: Loam-based No. 2 with 10 per cent added peat and soft sand.

Repotting: Once a year in spring but if plants are becoming leggy, repropagate from young tip cuttings. Pinch out the growing tips two or three times in summer to make a bushier plant. Large plants can also be divided in spring.

Cleaning: Spraying sufficient but if very dusty, flick with feather duster. No leafshine.

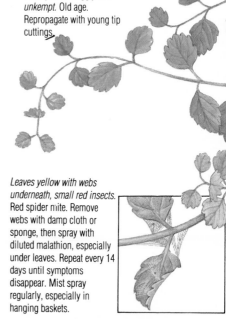

Plant grows straggly and unkempt. Old age. Repropagate with young tip cuttings.

Leaves yellow with webs underneath, small red insects. Red spider mite. Remove webs with damp cloth or sponge, then spray with diluted malathion, especially under leaves. Repeat every 14 days until symptoms disappear. Mist spray regularly, especially in hanging baskets.

Plant is limp and collapses. Too dry. Water immediately. Allow compost surface to just dry out before watering again. In winter water only once a week.

Leaves pale, plant grows slowly. Too dark. Move to window that does not get direct sun.

what goes wrong

Leaves dry and crisp. Damage by sunlight. Move into an area of diffused daylight, out of harmful rays of sun. Remove damaged leaf where it joins stem.

Leaves limp and drooping. Too hot. Move to cooler place, below 80°F (27°C). Spray twice weekly, especially in hot weather. If in window, shade from midday summer sun and spray in early morning or evening.

Leaves spotted with brown marks. Leafshine damage. Do not use. Clean only by spraying with soft tepid water. Remove damaged leaf where it joins main stem.

Mildew on stems, rot sets in. Botrytis. Plant too cold and damp. Spray with fungicide, then keep in warmer place (above 55°F, 13°C) and spray with water less frequently. Allow soil surface to dry out between waterings.

Leaves drop off while still green. Needs feeding. Feed with houseplant food at half maker's recommended strength every 21 days in the growing season, spring and summer.

Leaves turn yellow and drop off. Plant waterlogged, standing in water. Drain away any water in saucer and allow surface of soil to dry out before watering again. Then keep moist but never allow pot base to stand in water. Always throw away excess that drains through after watering.

Rhoeo discolor

Moses in the bullrushes

A pretty plant from Mexico that is closely related to the familiar Wandering Jew (Tradescantia). Unfortunately it is not so easy, and is really only suitable for someone with considerable experience of growing indoor plants. Its common name comes from the little white flowers which appear at the base of the leaves, half hidden in a boat-shaped bract. Great care must be taken with watering, especially in winter when overwatering can cause rotting. It grows first as a rosette of leaves but gradually produces a short stem, with the leaves and flowers growing on top. Offsets from around its base can be used to start new plants.

Moses in the bullrush plants are best treated as small specimen plants, that is, left to stand alone rather than planted together with others in a mixed bowl. They need careful watering, especially in winter, and soon rot if given too much at too low a temperature.

Light: Full light to partial shade. Keep out of midday summer sun.
Temperature: Winter minimum 60°F (16°C). In summer, ordinary room temperature, 70°F (21°C).
Water: Keep moist at all times watering 2–3 times a week in summer. In winter take great care particularly if temperature is near minimum. Water only once a week at most, with tepid (preferably soft) water. Always test compost.
Humidity: Spray at least twice weekly, summer and winter, more often if near maximum. In winter use tepid water.
Feeding: Every 14 days in spring and summer using liquid houseplant food at half maker's recommended strength.
Soil: Loam or peat-based No. 2.
Repotting: Once a year in spring when plant has outgrown its pot. If growth is slow leave to next year.
Cleaning: The spraying should keep it clean. Do not use leafshine.

Speckling or small burn marks all over plant. Leafshine damage. Do not use. Clean only by spraying with soft tepid water. Remove damaged leaf at base with sharp knife.

Leaves pale and plant looks tired. Not enough light. Move to a position in diffused daylight but not direct sun.

Small insects and webs under leaves. Red spider mite. Remove webs with damp cloth or sponge, then spray with diluted malathion, especially under leaves. Repeat every 14 days until symptoms disappear. Improve humidity by standing pot on saucer of wet pebbles and spray regularly.

Plant grows leggy and loses lower leaves. Old age. Propagate new plant from offshoots at base.

Plant becomes top heavy and won't stand up. Needs repotting. Move to larger pot and firm compost around base.

Propagation

1. When plant has flowered, offsets often grow around its base. When these are about 4in (10cm) tall, pull gently away, taking care not to damage their tiny roots.

2. Plant them in small pots containing drainage and compost of equal parts peat and sand. Leave in shade without water for 2 days, then treat as adult plants.

Leaf tips brown, leaves droop and curl. Soil and/or air too dry. Check compost and if dry, water well, then check compost regularly and keep moist in future. If over 70°F (21°C) spray daily.

what goes wrong

Brown marking on centre and edges of leaves. Damage caused by spraying in sunlight. Plant needs high humidity but must not be sprayed when sun is shining on it. Remove unsightly leaf at base with sharp knife.

Leaves curl inwards, darken and die. Too cold. Move to warmer place. Do not allow temperature to drop below 60°F (16°C).

Plant rots at stem. Compost too moist. Allow surface of soil to dry out before watering again. May need water 2–3 times a week in summer but not more than once a week in winter.

Mother-in-law's tongue

This is an easy plant which should be in everyone's collection as its leaf shape is strikingly different from most houseplants. It is very tolerant of most conditions except overwatering. If it is watered too much, especially in winter, the leaves may rot. Surprisingly, however, it does well in hydroculture (see p. 12). It has an interesting star-like yellow flower which grows on a stem rising straight up from the soil beside the leaves. This stem should be removed with a sharp knife when the flowers have died. Because of their special watering needs, they are difficult to use in mixed plantings unless the pot is isolated from the surrounding compost in an outer container of dry sand. The other plants around it can then be watered normally.

Mother-in-law's tongue has tall, spiky leaves with black markings in the centre and a band of cream at the edge. Occasionally all-green plants are seen but these are usually the result of propagating from cuttings. To maintain the cream markings, propagation must be by division.

Light: Flourishes in full sunlight but will survive in shade.
Temperature: Winter minimum 60°F (16°C) but will survive down to 50°F (10°C). In summer, normal room temperatures up to 75°F (24°C).
Water: Never overwater – if in doubt, don't water. About once a week in summer, only every 21 days in winter sufficient. Make sure drainage is good.
Humidity: Likes a dry atmosphere. Do not spray.
Feeding: Feed every 21 days in summer with liquid houseplant food at maker's recommended strength.
Soil: Loam-based No. 2.
Repotting: Prefers to be in a small pot and is best left until pot bursts. About every 2–3 years will do. Make sure compost is firmed down well around plant as it tends to become top-heavy and can fall over.

Leaf cuttings
1. Cut across base of healthy leaf with sharp knife and cut leaf into 1in (2½cm) sections. Make small slit in cut edges that were towards base.

2. Insert sections half into tray of sand, slit edge downwards.

3. Water well and cover. Keep at 70°F (21°C) until growing well. When they have 2 or 3 new leaves they can be lifted and repotted separately in small pots.

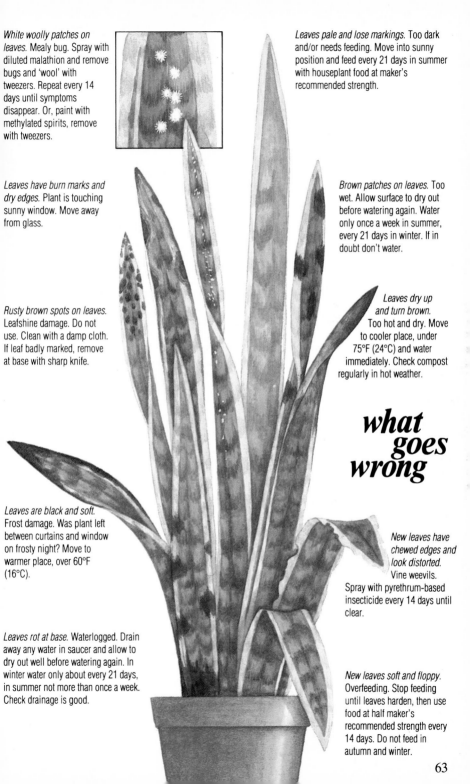

White woolly patches on leaves. Mealy bug. Spray with diluted malathion and remove bugs and 'wool' with tweezers. Repeat every 14 days until symptoms disappear. Or, paint with methylated spirits, remove with tweezers.

Leaves have burn marks and dry edges. Plant is touching sunny window. Move away from glass.

Rusty brown spots on leaves. Leafshine damage. Do not use. Clean with a damp cloth. If leaf badly marked, remove at base with sharp knife.

Leaves are black and soft. Frost damage. Was plant left between curtains and window on frosty night? Move to warmer place, over 60°F (16°C).

Leaves rot at base. Waterlogged. Drain away any water in saucer and allow to dry out well before watering again. In winter water only about every 21 days, in summer not more than once a week. Check drainage is good.

Leaves pale and lose markings. Too dark and/or needs feeding. Move into sunny position and feed every 21 days in summer with houseplant food at maker's recommended strength.

Brown patches on leaves. Too wet. Allow surface to dry out before watering again. Water only once a week in summer, every 21 days in winter. If in doubt don't water.

Leaves dry up and turn brown. Too hot and dry. Move to cooler place, under 75°F (24°C) and water immediately. Check compost regularly in hot weather.

what goes wrong

New leaves have chewed edges and look distorted. Vine weevils. Spray with pyrethrum-based insecticide every 14 days until clear.

New leaves soft and floppy. Overfeeding. Stop feeding until leaves harden, then use food at half maker's recommended strength every 14 days. Do not feed in autumn and winter.

63

Schefflera arboricola

Umbrella tree

Umbrella trees have increased in popularity over recent years as new varieties have been introduced, some more compact, some with attractive variegated leaves. Their larger relative, *Schefflera actinophylla*, grows to 8ft (2½m) tall with leaves up to 8in (20cm) long; but *S. arboricola* is a more manageable height, around 4ft (120cm) in a pot or tub. Often marketed under the alternative names *Heptapleurum* or *Brassaia* they are good plants to grow in hydroculture and are tolerant of less than perfect conditions in the home and office.

The Umbrella tree grows up to 4ft (120cm) tall and may make a foot (30cm) or more in a season. Its green or variegated leaves have about 7 leaflets which fall in a graceful umbrella shape over the stem. Smaller varieties are often available.

Light: Like most plants it prefers good indirect light with some morning sun but will tolerate a more shady position.
Temperature: Between 55–65°F (13–18°C) in winter; in summer normal room temperature, but increase ventilation if over 80°F (27°C).
Water: Keep moist, watering 2–3 times a week in summer, once a week in winter.
Humidity: Spray with soft water twice a week all year round. In dry, centrally-heated rooms, stand pot on saucer of wet pebbles for constant humidity.
Feeding: In summer, when growing, feed every 14 days with houseplant food diluted to half recommended strength.
Soil: Either loam or peat-based No. 2.
Repotting: Young plants need repotting twice a year as they grow up to a foot (30cm) a year. Older plants need repotting only once a year or every other year. When too large to handle easily, replace top 2–3in (5–7cm) soil in spring and feed regularly throughout the summer. Taller plants may need a cane. Insert when repotting, taking care not to damage roots.
Cleaning: Spraying will keep it clean. Use leafshine not more than once a month.

Variegated leaves lose colour. Too dark. Move into good indirect light; best with some sunlight every day but not direct midday sun.

Leaves have too few leaflets on young plant. These are the juvenile leaves, quite normal on young plant. Adult leaves have about 7 leaflets.

Cleaning
Spray leaves regularly for humidity and to keep them dust free. For extra shine, add liquid leafshine — but not more than once a month.

Plant becomes lanky with long spaces between leaves. Too hot. Move to a cooler, more airy place. Spray twice weekly with soft tepid water. If over 80°F (27°C) give fresh air.

White woolly patches on leaves and where leaves join stem. Mealy bug. Spray with diluted malathion and remove bugs and 'wool' with tweezers. Repeat every 14 days until symptoms disappear. Or, paint bugs with methylated spirits and remove with tweezers.

what goes wrong

Plant limp, leaves hang down. Too dry. Plunge pot into bucket of water for 10–15 minutes, then drain. Keep soil constantly moist in summer, watering every day if it dries out in hot weather. Do not allow to stand in water. Spray daily with soft tepid water.

Leaves pale or even yellow. Needs feeding. Feed with houseplant food diluted to half maker's recommended strength every 14 days in the growing season, spring and summer.

Brown scales on stems, leaf stalks and under leaves. Scale insect. Spray underside of leaves with diluted malathion and, after 48 hours, remove discs with thumbnail. Repeat every week for 4 weeks until clear.

Leaves distorted, and sticky with green insects. Greenfly. Spray with pyrethrum-based insecticide or diluted malathion. Repeat one week later and every week until clear.

Leaves yellow with webs underneath. Red spider mite. Remove webs with damp cloth or sponge, then spray with diluted malathion, especially under leaves. Repeat every 14 days until symptoms disappear. Improve humidity by standing pot on saucer of wet pebbles and spray regularly.

Leaves turn yellow, droop and fall. Too wet. Allow surface to dry out before watering again and check drainage in pot. Do not stand in water. If plant is cold, leaves may drop one by one while still green.

65

Devil's ivy

This distant relation of the Philoden-drons has similar habits and require-ments. It is good for both climbing and hanging positions: if grown as a climber it is best with a moss pole, for it has aerial roots which will cling to the moss. The size of the pointed, heart-shaped leaves increases dramati-cally as the plant gets older. Take care with watering. If given too much, especially in winter, the leaves may develop brown patches. Strangely, however, it grows well in hydroculture (p12). A vigorous climber, it will reach 15ft (over 4m) if allowed to grow unchecked. To keep it within bounds, prune back just above a leaf in spring.

Devil's ivy leaves have distinct yellow markings on a green background. If several plants are grown together in a hanging basket, preferably in a window that does not face the sun, they soon make an attractive display.

Light: Can be grown in semi-shade, though variegations fade if too dark. Keep out of direct sunlight.

Temperature: In winter best at 60°F (16°C) although it will survive down to 55°F (13°C). In summer keep below 75°F (24°C).

Water: Allow to dry out between waterings so good drainage is essential. Check com-post between waterings: every 4/5 days in summer, every 7/8 days in winter enough.

Humidity: Spray with water 2–3 times a week in summer. In winter if in dry, centrally heated room, spray twice a week with tepid water.

Feeding: Feed once a month all year round with liquid houseplant food at half maker's recommended strength.

Soil: Loam-based No. 2.

Repotting: Only every other year. They do not like roots to be disturbed. Make sure drainage is good.

Cleaning: Wipe leaves weekly with damp cloth, using vegetable oil about once a month to give them a shine. No leafshine.

Inserting a moss pole

1. Scindapsus has aerial roots which will grow into a moss pole. Insert pole when repotting, before placing plant in position. Add a handful of compost to keep it upright.

2. Position plant and tie to pole with raffia or twine, making sure knot is against pole, not stem.

3. Fill pot with fresh compost and press down well. When watering allow water to trickle down pole so that moss stays damp. This helps improve humidity and gives aerial roots moisture.

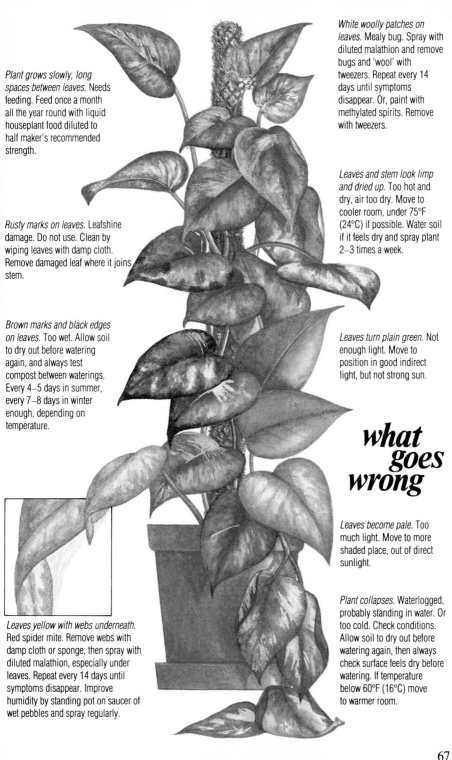

Plant grows slowly, long spaces between leaves. Needs feeding. Feed once a month all the year round with liquid houseplant food diluted to half maker's recommended strength.

White woolly patches on leaves. Mealy bug. Spray with diluted malathion and remove bugs and 'wool' with tweezers. Repeat every 14 days until symptoms disappear. Or, paint with methylated spirits. Remove with tweezers.

Leaves and stem look limp and dried up. Too hot and dry, air too dry. Move to cooler room, under 75°F (24°C) if possible. Water soil if it feels dry and spray plant 2–3 times a week.

Rusty marks on leaves. Leafshine damage. Do not use. Clean by wiping leaves with damp cloth. Remove damaged leaf where it joins stem.

Brown marks and black edges on leaves. Too wet. Allow soil to dry out before watering again, and always test compost between waterings. Every 4–5 days in summer, every 7–8 days in winter enough, depending on temperature.

Leaves turn plain green. Not enough light. Move to position in good indirect light, but not strong sun.

what goes wrong

Leaves become pale. Too much light. Move to more shaded place, out of direct sunlight.

Leaves yellow with webs underneath. Red spider mite. Remove webs with damp cloth or sponge, then spray with diluted malathion, especially under leaves. Repeat every 14 days until symptoms disappear. Improve humidity by standing pot on saucer of wet pebbles and spray regularly.

Plant collapses. Waterlogged, probably standing in water. Or too cold. Check conditions. Allow soil to dry out before watering again, then always check surface feels dry before watering. If temperature below 60°F (16°C) move to warmer room.

67

Mini bulrush

Bulrushes are a family of water-loving plants that thrive in bogs or on marshy land. This miniature variety can be used in aquariums as it will actually grow in water but is a good indoor pot plant as well and will last a long time if kept damp and in a humid atmosphere. Its grass-like leaves grow upright at first, then bend gracefully over, reaching 6–10in (13–25cm) long. It grows best in clay pots and is most attractive when quite small and young as it becomes untidy and straggly with age. Although the stems trail, the plant needs too much water to grow successfully in a hanging basket.

The grass-like stems of the miniature Bulrush plant produce tiny cream-coloured flowers at their tips. Though the stems trail gracefully, they are not really suitable for hanging baskets, since they need to grow in compost that is constantly very moist.

Light: Will stand full sun but better in indirect light. Will survive 4–6 weeks in a shady corner.

Temperature: Very tolerant, down to 45°F (8°C) in winter, though better around 55°F (13°C). If over 75°F (24°C), increase humidity.

Water: Moist at all times, summer and winter as it grows continuously unless temperature at minimum. Water 2–3 times a week all year round.

Humidity: Spray daily, twice a day in hot weather.

Feeding: Give liquid houseplant food every 3 weeks at maker's recommended strength while plant is growing. This may be all year round in normal room temperatures.

Soil: Loam-based No.2. Roots need firm compost.

Repotting: Every 6 months but best to divide plant into two rather than use a larger pot. Use clay pot if possible and make sure drainage is good.

Cleaning: Spraying should keep it clean. Leafshine spray can be used once a month but too frequent use will mark leaves.

Plant looks straggly, untidy and tired. Needs repotting and splitting in half. Small plants look more attractive than larger ones.

what goes wrong

Whole sections look burned, but still green on either side. Damage by sunlight. Move into an area of diffused daylight, out of harmful rays of sun. Remove damaged leaf.

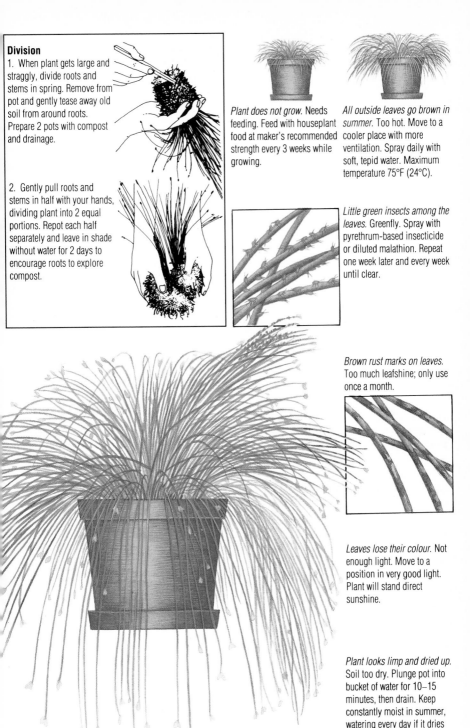

Division

1. When plant gets large and straggly, divide roots and stems in spring. Remove from pot and gently tease away old soil from around roots. Prepare 2 pots with compost and drainage.

2. Gently pull roots and stems in half with your hands, dividing plant into 2 equal portions. Repot each half separately and leave in shade without water for 2 days to encourage roots to explore compost.

Plant does not grow. Needs feeding. Feed with houseplant food at maker's recommended strength every 3 weeks while growing.

All outside leaves go brown in summer. Too hot. Move to a cooler place with more ventilation. Spray daily with soft, tepid water. Maximum temperature 75°F (24°C).

Little green insects among the leaves. Greenfly. Spray with pyrethrum-based insecticide or diluted malathion. Repeat one week later and every week until clear.

Brown rust marks on leaves. Too much leafshine; only use once a month.

Leaves lose their colour. Not enough light. Move to a position in very good light. Plant will stand direct sunshine.

Plant looks limp and dried up. Soil too dry. Plunge pot into bucket of water for 10–15 minutes, then drain. Keep constantly moist in summer, watering every day if it dries out in hot weather. Spray daily with soft tepid water.

69

Sonerila margaritacea

Pearl plant

A delightful but unfortunately delicate plant which is well worth trying to grow. It has small oval dark green leaves, covered with silvery dots which suggest pearl seeds, and reddish stems. The leaves are not more than 3in (7cm) long but are usually plentiful. It flowers briefly in the autumn with clusters of pretty little pink flowers but is attractive all the year round. It comes from Java and therefore likes warm moist conditions away from direct sunlight. It can be propagated from stem tip cuttings taken in spring and summer and rooted in a mixture of peat and sand. Since older plants tend to lose their lower leaves, it is wise to do this after 2 or 3 years if you want to keep an attractive, bushy plant.

The Pearl plant's seed-pearl markings make it a good plant to put in a mixed bowl, as a contrast to those with plainer green leaves. It also benefits from the extra humidity the other plants provide. If grown alone, it needs a moist, humid atmosphere.

Light: Does not like direct light and mid-day sun can kill. Best in partial shade.
Temperature: Winter minimum of 60°F (16°C). Below this leaves will drop. Summer maximum 75°F (24°C).
Water: Keep moist at all times, watering 2–3 times a week in summer, once a week in winter. Good drainage is essential.
Humidity: Likes a moist atmosphere. Spray every other day. Also if possible stand plant on saucer of wet pebbles.
Feeding: Every 14 days when growing in summer with liquid food at maker's recommended strength.
Soil: Loam-based No. 2.
Repotting: Once a year in spring, although as the plant tends to get rather leggy, it is often better to propagate new plants from cuttings than to pot up old plants.
Cleaning: The spraying should be enough. Do not use leafshine.

what goes wrong

Leaves curl, look dull and limp. Too hot. Move to cooler room, below 70°F (21°C) if possible and spray every other day.

Leaves drop off in winter. Too cold. Move to warmer place. Do not allow temperature to drop below 60°F (16°C).

Plant grows thin and straggly with small, pale leaves. Needs feeding. Feed with houseplant food diluted to maker's recommended strength every 14 days when growing in summer.

Leaves all over plant are limp. Compost and air too dry. Water immediately and spray regularly with water. Allow compost surface to just dry out before watering again. In winter water only once a week, but spray regularly.

Plant collapses. Waterlogged, standing in water. Drain away any water in saucer and allow surface of soil to dry out before watering again. Then keep moist but never allow pot base to stand in water. Always throw away excess that drains through after watering.

Plant grows tall and leggy with no bottom leaves. Old age. Repropagate from stem tip cuttings.

Little red insects under leaves. Red spider mite. Remove webs with damp cloth or sponge, then spray with diluted malathion, especially under leaves. Repeat every 14 days until symptoms disappear. Improve humidity.

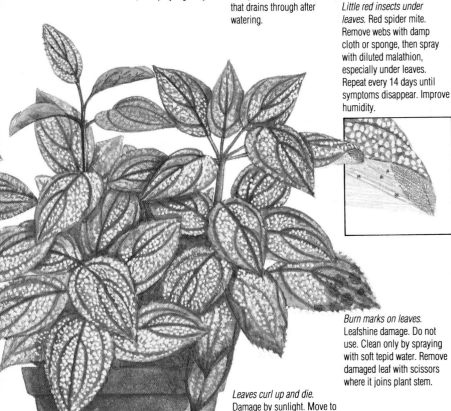

Burn marks on leaves. Leafshine damage. Do not use. Clean only by spraying with soft tepid water. Remove damaged leaf with scissors where it joins plant stem.

Leaves curl up and die. Damage by sunlight. Move to an area of diffused daylight, out of harmful rays of sun. Remove damaged leaf.

Sparmannia africana

Indoor lime tree

The indoor lime is a very beautiful plant which makes a splendid feature in a room. Unfortunately it is not as widely available as it deserves to be – but is well worth asking for. It needs plenty of light but tolerates quite low temperatures. A native of South Africa, it may produce clusters of white flowers with purple stamens, when over 3 years old, especially if it is kept slightly pot-bound. If it is growing too big for the available space, it can be pruned in spring. Use secateurs and cut at an angle just above a leaf or side branch. Dust cut with sulphur dust to protect from any. infection. It grows quickly and will need a strong cane to support it and a heavy pot.

The leaves of the elegant Indoor lime are like those of the outdoor lime tree in shape, and are delicate green covered with fine hairs. It does not need high temperatures but good light is essential for healthy growth. In ideal conditions it will grow to 6ft (2m) in a pot or tub.

Light: Good natural light, but midday sun in summer may burn the leaves.
Temperature: In winter down to 45°F (7°C) if soil allowed to dry out completely between waterings. Summer maximum 75°F (24°C).
Water: In summer, never allow to dry out, watering 3 times a week. In winter water once a week unless below 50°F (10°C), when every 10 days is sufficient.
Humidity: Spray 2–3 times a week in summer, but not when sun is on leaves.
Feeding: Add liquid houseplant food to the water every 14 days in spring and summer, diluting to maker's recommended strength.
Soil: Loam-based No. 3, a rich soil.
Repotting: It grows quickly, so repot at least twice during first year. After this, repot once a year in spring. If not repotted for 3 years, then fed weekly, plant should flower.
Cleaning: Dust lightly with feather duster – leaves and young stems break easily. No leafshine.

Rusty marks on leaves. Leafshine damage. Do not use. Clean by carefully dusting with feather duster. Remove damaged leaf where it joins stem.

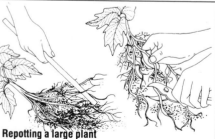

Repotting a large plant
1. A large plant can be replaced in its original pot with fresh compost. Wait until soil is dry, then remove plant and lay on flat surface covered with paper. Remove old compost with stick.

2. Prune longest roots with secateurs. Wash out pot, fill with fresh compost and replace plant. Leave in shade without water for 2 days to recover.

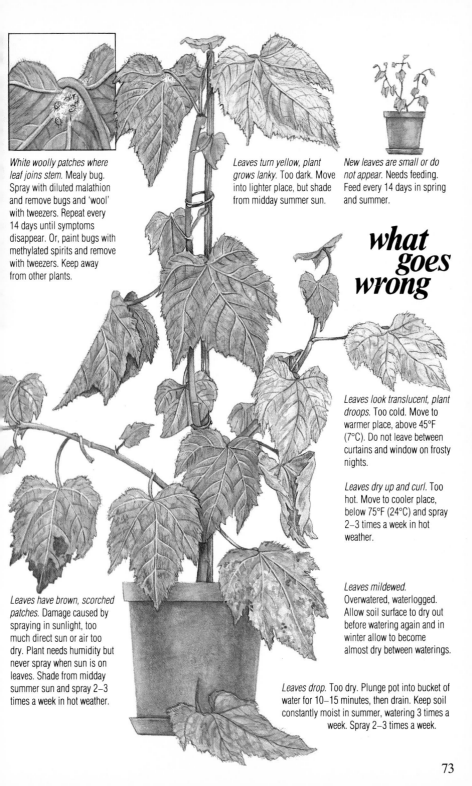

White woolly patches where leaf joins stem. Mealy bug. Spray with diluted malathion and remove bugs and 'wool' with tweezers. Repeat every 14 days until symptoms disappear. Or, paint bugs with methylated spirits and remove with tweezers. Keep away from other plants.

Leaves turn yellow, plant grows lanky. Too dark. Move into lighter place, but shade from midday summer sun.

New leaves are small or do not appear. Needs feeding. Feed every 14 days in spring and summer.

what goes wrong

Leaves look translucent, plant droops. Too cold. Move to warmer place, above 45°F (7°C). Do not leave between curtains and window on frosty nights.

Leaves dry up and curl. Too hot. Move to cooler place, below 75°F (24°C) and spray 2–3 times a week in hot weather.

Leaves mildewed. Overwatered, waterlogged. Allow soil surface to dry out before watering again and in winter allow to become almost dry between waterings.

Leaves have brown, scorched patches. Damage caused by spraying in sunlight, too much direct sun or air too dry. Plant needs humidity but never spray when sun is on leaves. Shade from midday summer sun and spray 2–3 times a week in hot weather.

Leaves drop. Too dry. Plunge pot into bucket of water for 10–15 minutes, then drain. Keep soil constantly moist in summer, watering 3 times a week. Spray 2–3 times a week.

Stenocarpus sinuatus

False oak

A good houseplant which will stand a wide range of temperatures and conditions, the False oak has been sadly neglected by the nursery trade. In its native Queensland it grows up to 100ft (30m) but indoors in a pot or tub is usually no more than 6ft (2m). The leaves, which look like large glossy oak leaves, are its main attraction, growing up to 18in (30cm) long. In a conservatory or large greenhouse it will produce clusters of bright red flowers but these only appear on mature specimens too large for most homes. Unless the growing tip is removed it usually grows as a single main stem.

Young False oak leaves are reddish in colour, changing gradually to green as they mature. If a branching tree is desired, it is best to pinch out the growing tip in summer to encourage side shoots to push out further down the stem.

Light: Flourishes in good light but protect from midday summer sun. A good conservatory plant.

Temperature: Down to 40°F (4°C) in winter, normal room temperatures in summer. If over 75°F (24°C) give plenty of fresh air.

Water: Keep soil always moist unless temperature below 50°F (10°C), when soil should dry out between watering. Twice a week in summer, once a week in winter adequate.

Humidity: Spray twice weekly all year.

Feeding: Feed every 14 days in growing season with liquid houseplant food at maker's recommended strength.

Soil: Loam-based No. 2 compost. Needs to be well rooted.

Repotting: Twice a year when young and growing rapidly. After 3–4 years, when too large to handle easily, replace top 2–3in (5–7cm) with fresh compost. Always firm plant well into compost.

Cleaning: Regular spraying will keep it clean but leafshine can be used once a month for extra gloss.

White woolly patches where leaf joins stem. Mealy bug. Spray with diluted malathion and remove bugs and 'wool' with tweezers. Repeat every 14 days until symptoms disappear. Or, paint bugs with methylated spirits and remove with tweezers. Keep away from other plants.

Support
False Oaks may need to be supported with a cane when young. Insert this when repotting, after adding first layer of compost but before positioning plant. If adding at any other time, push gently into compost a few inches away from stem being careful not to damage roots. Tie loosely to stem.

74

Growth stops in summer. Needs feeding. Feed every 14 days with houseplant food at maker's recommended strength.

Leaves bleached. Too much light. Move to more shady place, out of direct sun.

Spot marks on leaves which turn into burn holes. Damage caused by spraying in sunlight. Plant needs high humidity but must not be sprayed when sun is shining on it or droplets will act like magnifying glasses and burn leaves. Remove unsightly leaf where it joins main stem.

Leaves go pale, stem is lanky and plant looks tired. Not enough light. Move to a position in diffused daylight, not full sun.

Leaves drop while still green. Too cold. Move to warmer place, at least 40°F (4°C).

Leaves discoloured with webs underneath. Red spider mite. Remove webs with damp cloth or sponge, then spray with diluted malathion, especially under leaves. Repeat every 14 days until symptoms disappear. Spray regularly.

Leaves dry up. Too hot. If temperature over 80°F (27°C) give fresh air. Move to cooler place if possible and spray regularly.

Green insects and sticky substance on and under leaves. Greenfly. Spray with pyrethrum-based insecticide or diluted malathion. Repeat one week later and every week until clear.

what goes wrong

Leaves drop. Soil too dry. Plunge pot into bucket of water for 10–15 minutes then drain. Keep soil constantly moist in summer, watering every day if it dries out in hot weather. Do not allow to stand in water.

Leaves yellow and fall. Too wet. Check not standing in water. If below 50°F (10°C), allow soil to dry out between waterings. If soil waterlogged, allow to dry out before watering again, then always check compost, especially in cold weather.

75

Yucca elephantipes

Spineless yucca

These are interesting and easy plants to keep in the home, and less dangerous indoors than the other indoor yucca, the spiky *Yucca aloifolia*. Canes between 1 and 5ft (30–90cm) are imported from the West Indies, forced into growth in a greenhouse and, when they have a good head of green, potted singly or two or three together. When canes of different heights are potted together they make an attractive display. Always make sure that the plant you buy is well rooted in its pot. Yucca canes will not grow taller but more leaves will grow from each rosette.

Yuccas make a handsome display, especially if canes of different heights are planted together. The leaves of this species are not dangerous, bending easily at the touch of a finger, but the spiky *Yucca aliofolia* has leaves that are dangerously sharp.

Light: Need good light including sunlight except at midday in summer. Will survive for 4–5 weeks in a shady place. Can be put outside in summer.

Temperature: Keep between 50–60°F (10–16°C) in winter; normal room temperature in summer or outdoors on a balcony or patio.

Water: Keep moist in summer, watering every 2–3 days if soil seems to be drying out. In winter every 10 days should be enough.

Humidity: In summer spray once or twice a week; once a month in winter unless over 65°F (18°C), when weekly spraying will keep them fresh.

Feeding: Feed weekly in summer using liquid houseplant food at half maker's recommended strength.

Soil: Loam-based No. 2.

Repotting: Once a year when young. After 3–4 years, remove top 2–3in (5–7cm) compost and replace with new. Always firm compost well down around base of cane, especially with tall plants.

Cleaning: Wipe leaves carefully with damp cloth. No leafshine.

White woolly patches in centre of leaves. Mealy bug. Spray with diluted malathion and remove bugs and 'wool' with tweezers. Repeat every 14 days until symptoms disappear. Or, paint bugs with methylated spirits and remove with tweezers. Keep away from other plants.

what goes wrong

Rosettes (especially young ones) turn black and rot. Too wet. Allow surface to dry out before watering again. Water 2–3 times a week in summer, only once every 10 days in winter.

76

A yucca garden
1. Choose 3 plants of different heights and a pot large enough to hold them with at least 3in (8cm) between for root growth. Pot must be heavy or it may be unstable.

2. Remove plants from pots and position first one in compost. Firm well in. Add second and third plants around it, firming compost well round them. Fill pot with compost and leave in shade without water for 2 days.

Brown scales under leaves and on stems. Scale insect. Spray underside of leaves with diluted malathion and, after 48 hours, remove scales with thumbnail. Repeat every week for 4 weeks until clear. Or, paint scales with methylated spirits and remove with thumbnail.

Grey mould on leaves. Botrytis. Too cold and damp. Spray with fungicide, then move plant to warmer room (over 50°F, 10°C) and spray less often. Allow soil to dry out in winter between waterings.

Rusty marks on leaves. Leafshine damage. Do not use. Clean with damp cloth if dusty.

Leaves pale. Too much direct sun. Need good light but while indoors keep out of midday summer sun. Outdoors will stand full sun.

Leaves dry up in winter. Too hot. Keep at 50–60°F (10–18°C) in winter. If temperature over 65°F (18°C) spray weekly.

Lower leaves yellow. Too dark. Move to lighter place, plant will stand full sun. Remove yellow leaves with sharp knife where they join cane.

Plant falls over. Not sufficiently rooted in pot. Replace carefully in pot and firm soil well down around base of cane. Place in full light to encourage root growth.

New leaves do not grow. Needs feeding or, if feeding regular, too cold. Check conditions. Feed weekly in summer with houseplant food at half maker's recommended strength and keep above 50°F (10°C) in winter.

77

Zebrina pendula

Wandering sailor

These attractive plants look very like the familiar 'Wandering Jew' (Trades-cantias) and are closely related to them, but with larger and stronger leaves. They flourish in good light, which brings out the bright purple and cream of their leaves. If in too shady a position, or in winter when the days are short, the leaves may turn almost green. But when better conditions return, the bright colours reappear. They are at their most attractive massed in a hanging basket in a good, light position. If stem tips are regularly replanted, the pot will be kept full and bushy, with no bare, brown stems visible. Remember to check the compost regularly in hanging pots and baskets, as they dry out quickly. A layer of damp pebbles or gravel in the drip tray will help provide humidity.

The colouring of the Wandering sailor plant's leaves improves in good light. They are best in a hanging basket where 3 or 4 pots together provide a mass of purple trailing stems.

Light: Must have plenty of light, including full sunlight except at midday in summer.
Temperature: Winter minimum 55°F (13°C). In summer normal room temperature, but best below 70°F (21°C).
Water: Keep moist all year round. Water twice a week in summer, once a week in winter.
Humidity: Like humid atmosphere. Stand pot on wet pebbles all year round.
Feeding: Add liquid houseplant food to water every 14 days in spring and summer, diluting to maker's recommended strength.
Soil: Loam-based No. 2.
Repotting: Best to repropagate every 2nd or 3rd year instead of repotting, as they become straggly with age. Root 4 or 5 cuttings in a 3in (7cm) pot, repot after 6 months into 5in (13cm) pot, then leave.
Cleaning: Spray if dusty with tepid water. No leafshine.

Propagation
1. When plant looks bare at base, cut off 3–4in (5–7cm) length from stem tip, including at least 2 pairs of leaves and the growing tip. Cut just below a leaf or joint.

2. Trim to just below leaves, then remove lowest pair and insert stem end in small pot of fresh compost. Keep moist and new growth will show in 2–3 weeks.

Stems grow straggly with long spaces between leaves. Too dark. Move into lighter place, but not direct sun.

78

Burn marks on leaves.
Leafshine damage or too
much direct midday sun. Do
not use leafshine: clean only
by spraying with soft tepid
water if dusty. Remove
damaged leaf where it joins
stem. Keep plant in good
indirect light.

Leaves lose markings and
grow thickly. Overfeeding.
Dilute food to half
recommended strength. Feed
only every 14 days.

Stems rot at base.
Waterlogged, standing in
water. Drain away any water in
saucer and allow surface to
dry out before watering again.
Always throw away excess
water from saucer after
watering.

what goes wrong

Leaves distorted with sticky
green insects. Greenfly. Spray
with pyrethrum-based
insecticide or diluted
malathion. Repeat weekly
until clear.

Leaves curl, webs underneath.
Red spider mite. Remove
webs with damp cloth or
sponge, then spray with
diluted malathion, especially
under leaves. Repeat every 14
days until symptoms
disappear. Improve humidity.

Leaves curl inwards, then dry
up. Too hot, air too dry, or too
cold. Check conditions. If
over 75°F (24°C) move to
cooler more airy place.
Improve humidity and keep
over 55°F (13°C).

Leaves soft and discoloured.
Much too cold, possibly
frosted. Repropagate from
healthy stem tips.

Brown tips and patches on
leaves. Too dry. Keep moist
all year round.

Plant is straggly, stems bare
at base, falling out of pot.
Needs repotting or cut stems
back to 3in (7cm) from pot so
that they will grow new
leaves. Or propagate from
stem tips.

79

Buying your houseplant

Florists, garden centres and specialist shops are best for unusual plants, large specimens and planted arrangements. Supermarkets, stores and service stations often offer excellent value in popular plants and rely on fast turnover to maintain quality. Market stalls may appear to offer good value but take care, especially in winter, when cold may affect the plants badly.

It is important before buying to consider where the plant is to go. Think about the room conditions, the light, heat or draughts that the plant may be subjected to. If you are a beginner choose a plant that is simple to grow. Don't be tempted to buy one that is exotic until you have had some experience.

Look carefully at the one you intend to buy. It should be firm in its pot, which should be clean. The compost on top should be fresh, not sprouting weeds or moss. None of the leaves should be marked, torn, yellow or faded. Beware of small plants in large pots; this probably means that they have just been repotted and the roots will not have grown properly into the fresh compost.

Always insist, particularly in winter, that the plant you buy is properly wrapped up, if necessary with a double layer of paper. Large plants often require support, with an extra cane to protect the growing tip. Take care not to knock it on the way home.

Lastly, make sure you know the plant's correct name so that you can look up its care instructions when you get home. Common names vary from place to place; the scientific name is the most reliable to use for identification.

Acknowledgements

Colour artwork by Jane Fern/The Garden Studio (pp. 15, 19, 21, 27, 29, 37, 39, 41, 51, 55, 61, 63, 65, 67, 71, 77, 79). Stuart Lafford/Linden Artists Ltd (pp. 17, 25, 35, 45, 59, 69, 75). Jane Pickering/Linden Artists (pp. 31, 49, 57, 73). Norman Barber/Linden Artists Ltd (pp. 23, 47, 53). Andrew Riley/The Garden Studio (pp. 43). Lisa Horstman/The Garden Studio (pp. 33)

Line artwork by Norman Bancroft-Hunt, Patricia Newton

Photographs by David Cockroft

Additional photographs supplied by The Harry Smith Horticultural Photographic Collection and A–Z Botanical Photographic Collection

Designed by Marion Neville

Typeset by Oxford Publishing Services